Dear Bethy…

Dear Frosty…

The Wartime Letters

Between

Frank and Bethine Church

Bethine and Frank Church at the family home in Boise @1980.

Dear Bethy...
Dear Frosty...

The Wartime Letters Between Frank and Bethine Church

edited by Garry V. Wenske

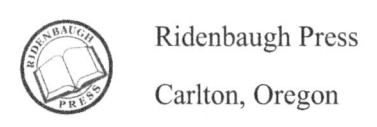

Ridenbaugh Press
Carlton, Oregon

DEAR BETHY ... DEAR FROSTY ...
The Wartime Letters Between Frank and Bethine Church
Copyright ©2024 by The Frank Church Institute
All rights reserved. No part of this book may be reproduced or transmitted in any form, by any information storage or retrieval system, without written permission from the publisher, except in case of brief quotations used in critical articles or reviews.
For more information, contact Ridenbaugh Press, P.O. Box 834, Carlton OR 97111.
Printed and bound in the United States of America.
First edition July 2024
10 9 8 7 6 5 4 3 2 1

Library of Congress Cataloging in Publication Data

Frank Church, Bethine Church

Dear Bethy... Dear Frosty...

Bibliography

1. History. 2. Idaho Politics and Government.

I. Church, Frank. II. Title.

ISBN 978-0-945648-56-7 (softbound)

Ridenbaugh Press
P.O. Box 834, Carlton OR 97111
Phone (503) 852-0010
www.ridenbaugh.com
stapilus@ridenbaugh.com

Photographs courtesy Frank Church Papers, Boise State University Special Collections and Archives.

Foreword

Long-time Senator Frank Church of Idaho is well remembered in the state and nation four decades after his death and longer than that since he left the U.S. Senate.

He was a major public figure, immediately the center of attention wherever he went – whether drawing a response of praise or criticism. A serious candidate for president around the time he was most influential, Frank Church was an important public figure in every sense.

That means among other things that many people who read of him or heard him or knew him even slightly in passing – as I did, covering him for several years as a newspaper reporter during his final Senate term and campaign – probably had the sense that they "knew" him, had a feel for who he was and what he was about.

Like most politicians, Church cultivated that. Politicians prefer not to be mysterious; voters are uncomfortable with what they don't know (or *know* they don't know), and most vote-gatherers try to clearly define themselves. In running for president in 2020 Joe Biden remarked, "You know me" – a reflection both of his long political career, but also in a callout to the idea that voters would have a comforting sense of who he was.

That self-crafted definition of personality, of course, is only ever part of the story. Every person is complex, and every politician shows only a part of the picture, at least willingly.

This book, *Dear Bethy... Dear Frosty...*, of course does not tell the whole story of the Churches. But it does add to what's already widely known and what has been reported in biography, memoir and other accounts. It consists of letters – which survive and have made their way into the Church papers in the collection at Boise State University – between the two of them in the period just before America's entry into World War II into the days just before their marriage in 1947. (They had less need to send lengthy letters to each other after that.) It includes the years of Church's military service in Asia and part of his time as a law student at Stanford University.

What gives these letters an entirely new look at the Churches (both of them, after all, became highly public figures) is their personal nature. These letters were not intended, when written, to be seen by anyone but the recipient. Some of them seem almost startlingly personal – there were points in reading them that I had the uncomfortable feeling of eavesdropping on a very private conversation. There are also large gaps, which in places the reader will have to creatively fill in.

But they also are letters of two people just beginning their adult lives, finding their way in the world and thinking seriously about it. There is no hint here of immediate political planning or positioning; if Church was clearly an ambitious young man even then (and he was) his ambitions seem uncertain and vague. He intended to become a lawyer and probably get into politics in some way, but the details weren't yet in place while these letters were made. These letters were written with no larger audience in mind.

The letters also throw new light on the private people they were, and on their relationships with friends. The path of courtship of Frank Church and Bethine Clark was not simple and not without some strain and conflict, something that seems almost hard to grasp for those of us who knew them in later years.

One of Church's closest friends during all his political adventures – a boyhood friend – was Carl Burke, who became a Boise attorney and manager of Church's campaigns. But these letters make clear that things weren't always so smooth-running: For a period of two years or more during the war, the two were n the outs and hardly willing to communicate; the letters do not indicate why.

Throw light in one new place in a person's life, and new mysteries bloom.

But our level of understanding increases anyway.

Reading these letters may, for many people, have another kind of effect, less political and historical. In this new century traditional letter writing has faded as most people are more readily able to communicate in other ways. But until this digital age, letters seny often at long distance often were the only way people could keep in touch.

It was a cumbersome way of doing that, but it could force both clarity and eloquence; if writing the words on paper is the only way to make an important communication, some care with those words is apt to be taken. So it was with the Churches, and so it was too with the many other people in similar positions. Many of us have forebears who sent communications like these, and for many of us they open windows into worlds we otherwise might never know.

These letters tell a human story of not political stick figures, but of people, in a way no less relevant to us almost a century later.

Randy Stapilus

Publisher, Ridenbaugh Press

Introduction

"Bethy" and "Frosty" were the affectionate names Senator Frank and Bethine Church called each other in private. Some of their letters to each other during World War II survived and are housed at the Frank Church Collection at Boise State University.

Their letters, sometimes deeply personal, and other times revealing Frank's prescience about his future role world affairs, foreshadow their becoming full partners in life and politics.

Both the Churches were born into Idaho pioneer families. The first Frank Forrester Church settled in Idaho City in 1872 where he was appointed United States Assayer for Idaho by President Grover Cleveland. Bethine Clark's family homesteaded the Robinson Bar ranch near Mackay on the Salmon River. Bethine was the daughter of Governor and then Federal Judge Chase Clark appointed by President Franklin Roosevelt; niece of Governor Barzilla Clark; and cousin of Congressman and then Senator D. Worth Clark.

After first meeting as students at Boise High School where he was elected student body president, Frank and Bethine were destined for something larger.

That opportunity first came in 1941 when Frank won the American Legion National Oratorical Contest and a $4,000 scholarship, which allowed him to attend to attend Stanford University.

Following Pearl Harbor during Frank's freshman year, he enrolled as an officer in the U.S. Army where he served as a military intelligence officer in China.

After the war, he returned to Stanford where he also received a law degree and was awarded the Joffre Medal for his debating skills. As a law student he also battled a serious cancer, which taught him that life was tenuous, and that he must take big risks to make a difference.

His survival gave him the courage to run for the U.S. Senate, where at age 32, he became one of the youngest Senators in U.S. history and served four terms.

Over 24 years, Frank Church became a leading Senator shaping U.S. foreign policy; ending the Vietnam War; reigning in U.S. intelligence agencies; protecting America's wild lands and rivers; and championing the rights of senior citizens. In 1976, he launched a long-shot race for President and defeated the eventual nominee in five primaries.

For every campaign for Senate, as well as for President, and for every major issue in the Senate, Frank and Bethine became partners in life and politics, and she became known as "Idaho's Third Senator."

After the Senator's untimely death in 1984, Bethine established the Frank Church Institute, together with the Frank and Bethine Church Chair of Public Policy; and the Frank Church Scholarships at Boise State University. She also founded the Sawtooth Society to protect the Stanley Basin surrounded by the Sawthooths, Idaho's crown jewels.

Biographies of Senator Church titled "Fighting the Odds" and "The Last Honest Man," and Bethine Church's memoirs, titled "A

Lifelong Affair: My Passion for People and Politics," bookend their remarkable partnership. They represent America's greatest generation who devoted their lives to public service and whose legacies continue to inspire future generations.

Garry V. Wenske

Emeritus Executive Director

The Frank Church Institute

Boise State University

The Letters

"President Roosevelt moves again to range United States aid behind Britain's war effort."

N.Y. Times 4/12/1941

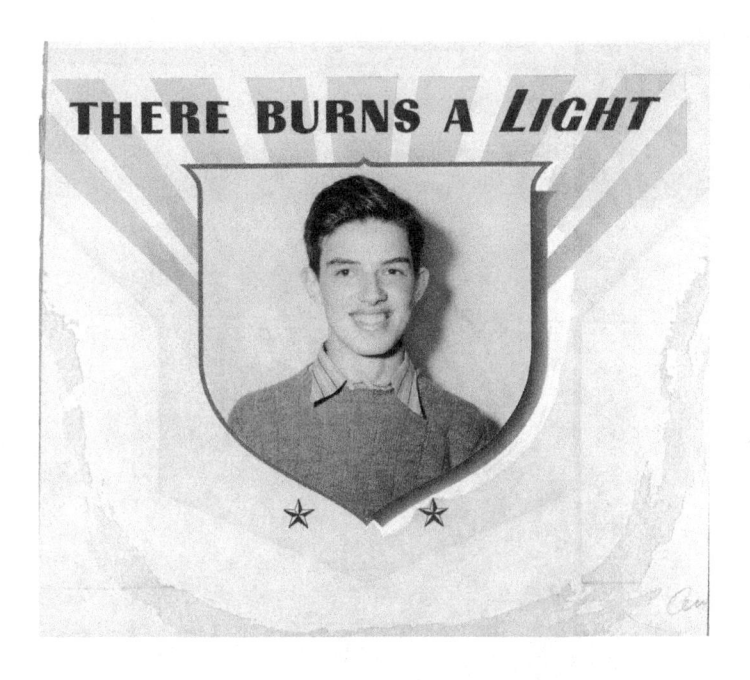

Frank Church at the American Legion National Oratorical Contest in South Carolina where he won first place and a $4,000 scholarship in 1941.

Cheyenne, WY
April 12, 1941

Dear Bethy,

Thanks a million for your telegram. Both yours and your father's helped greatly in giving me the encouragement to win. Cross your fingers and wish me luck next Tuesday.

Frank.

Frank Church in his Boise High School R.O.T.C. uniform. Both Frank Church and Carl Burke were members of the Boise High School R.O.T.C. Church was commissioned in the Army as a 2nd Lt., while Burke (whose father was chairman of the

Selective Service board in Boise) was drafted and served throughout the War as a private in Europe where he was awarded a purple heart.

"*In Tokyo, government, military and naval authorities continued conferences to decide Japan's course.*"

N.Y. Times 6/27/1941

San Diego, CA
June 27, 1941

Dear Bethine,

Although I don't know when you will read this, I wanted to write and tell you that everything is under control, and I am seeing many interesting sights.

Love, Frank.

"*An important gain on the Far Eastern wing of the Axis offensive was reported yesterday.*"

N.Y. Times 7/24/1941

Warm Lake, ID
July 24, 1941

My dearest Bethy,

For over a week I have waited patiently for a letter. Now it becomes plain that I must write first. Well, fair enough!....

That's all the news for now except to say that I miss you greatly and hope you are enjoying every minute of your vacation.

Love, Frank.

p.s. Have you heard the latest true story out of the war?...it follows:

Shortly after the First World War, the German High Command, investigating the reasons for their defeat, decided that the "Tommies" staying power was largely because of their sense of humor. One of the jokes showed "Old Bill" sitting at his desk over which was an immense hole. A rookie asked "what did it?" and Old Bill replied, "a mouse." Underneath a solemn foot note explained, "It wasn't a mouse, it was a shell."

p.p.s. tomorrow I am 17.

"Speculation over a possible second front found new fuel in London."

N.Y. Times 7/31/1942

**Green R. & Port. MD
July 31, 1942**

Dear Bethy,

Your letter just arrived. It was great! Everyone enjoyed it tremendously. I haven't time now to write so I'll drop this note to tell you that the date set for a week from Saturday suits swell. Plan on it and think of me in the heat.

Love, Frank.

"Allied military experts began yesterday taking stock…. as new details emerged from that dress rehearsal for a second front….Another report of a successful Allied Action in the Far East came from the Chinese."

N.Y. Times 8/21/1942

Frank Church, Carl Burke and Boise High School friends.

August 21, 1942

Dear Bethy

Thanks so much for your letter, Bethy, and especially for the "secret" note. You are absolutely right! Things are to nearly at a climax to let anything, however small, tint the happy memories. The status quo was not nearly as tense as you had imagined, luckily enough…

Now, young lady, since you won't be around next Saturday I want to sign you up for a royal engagement of rollicking laughter and fun the following Saturday evening. Contract is signed and sealed and it will be considered illegal to breach any provisions therein contained, etc. etc..

Tonight is a night for celebration. Just one week from now I shall again be a free man. And then----Oh, what a wonderful time I shall have for many a dime. Until then and particularly when reminded by the heat, remember me slaving away for Chase [Bethine's father Gov. Chase Clark] for Idaho, for the public welfare-------and for a salary!!!

Yours ever in love and kisses,

Frank Forrester Church Junior the III, Esq.

[The graves of Bethine and Senator Frank Church III, along with his father, Frank Church II, his grandfather Frank Church, and his son Frank Church IV are in Boise's Morris Hill Cemetery].

> *"Secretary of War Stimson landed in England yesterday and immediately set off speculation concerning further assaults on the Axis."*
>
> N.Y. Times 7/12/1943

Frank Church at Lafayette College. Church volunteered for the U.S. Army on December 7, 1942 when he was sent to Lafayette College, PA for officer candidate school.

Easton, PA
July 12, 1943

Dearest Bethine,

Having just received your letter, and having secured the Robinson Bar [the Clark homestead on the Salmon River] picture on the mirror above the bureau, I sit down to write my thanks in the few minutes remaining before taps.

At last I am settled, and ready to begin work. The surroundings here are conducive to study for Lafayette College fairly breathes "atmosphere." Classes began today. The college is situated on the top of the dominating hill above Easton [PA], a town about the size of Boise. It is closed away by many hundreds of trees making the whole scene beautiful.

I am studying Spanish only as a language, with two hours of conversation a day. This afternoon the professor conducted his entire period in Spanish. He asked questions, made grammatical explanations, assignments, and suggestions without a word of English. So it will be from own on out. Most of the men are much older and far more experienced in languages than myself. I just hope for the breaks.

Just where we Spanish students will fit in, in not clear. We are studying the geography, history, economics, etc. of France, Italy and Germany, nations to be occupied after the battle ends. But what is in the offing for Spanish language, nobody knows. Possibly not even the government! Nevertheless, my day begins at 5:30 and ends at 10:30 in the evening. What a grind!

As for the three-day pass (we were informed that only 15% of the men will get seven-day furloughs), it will come sometime in October. Let's plan ahead anyway. I am just 73 miles from New York, but several hundred from Michigan. [Bethine Church transferred to the University of Michigan after attending Boise Junior College]. I tell you, Bethy, there's just no luck in this man's army.

Taps have just sounded. Please write often. I'm anxious for the picture.

Good night and love,

Frosty

The Fascists surrendered their control over Italy yesterday when Premier Mussolini quit…

The Fourteenth United States Air Force in China beat off four waves of more than 100 planes when the Japanese attacked advanced American bases in Hunan Province.

N.Y. Times 7/26/1943

APO New York, N.Y.
July 1943

Dear Bethy,

The press of activity can be blamed for the interval of silence. Hope my last letter reached you in San Francisco. High hopes for being home before Christmas!

Frosty.

The Army and Navy Journal declared editorially that President Roosevelt, in his message to Congress this week, would ask for a national service act conscripting all men and women into the war effort.

N.Y. Times 1/9/1944

Frank Church at Camp Ritchie MD. The "Ritchie Boys" was a term used for American soldiers who trained at Camp Ritchie during World War II. At Camp Ritchie MD, military instructors taught intelligence-gathering collections and analysis to approximately 20,000 soldiers.

Camp Ritchie, MD
9 January 1944

Dear Bethy,

There are two boxes of stationery on my desk. One very fat box filled with thick, inferior paper is for ordinary correspondence. The other box is much lighter. It holds a "Air Mail" paper especially for use when letters are to be written which are inexcusably tardy. I reached first for the former, and then for the latter, remembering that I had promised to write after arriving home. But I'm afraid, despite the fact that putting an eight cent stamp on a letter that would otherwise go free is a tribute worthwhile, that I am nonetheless very guilty.

I had intended to make this past leave a care free, happy, memorable last fling. It turned out to be even more fun that I had anticipated. Of all the many good times I had, I'll remember our evening in Detroit, the dancing, the dining, the laughs, and the music,--- the effortless happiness. Thanks millions, Bethy, for so grand a time.

My visit home was as quiet as it was satisfying. Boise is vacant. Outside of Wade, Helen …. a few other close friends, and the family, I found myself in the midst of strangers. The effects of war are marked indeed when a person feels like a transient in his own home town.

You can imagine, Bethy, how busy I've been since returning. No changes in prospect, and I'm glad for that. Packing, formations, written forms, inoculations, and all kinds of administrative details are the order of every day. Yesterday, my enlisted men were promoted and equipment was issued as that I have now taken over my first command.

Although I'll be unable to write for some time, Bethy, please continue to write at this address. My mail will be forwarded. When my new address is assigned, you will receive a postal care to that effect.

HAPPY NEW YEAR!

With love, Frosty

American destroyers sailed into the Japanese base [in] New Guinea, and in cooperation with fighter planes and bombers, left the place gutted."

N.Y. Times 4/12/1944

Fort Benning, GA
April 12, 1944

Dear Bethy,

Every time I want to write a real personal letter to you I stumble onto a typewriter and, knowing no better, I can't resist the temptation of using it. I always do a little better on the typewriter so don't let the cold formality of black print obscure the very deep personal feelings that accompany this letter.

Shortly after receiving your letter, I had a long talk with a buddy of mine, an older married man, who sleeps on the next bunk adjoining mine. This is the story I told him. I tell it now to you because I think it can best clarify the way I feel and have felt for many months.

"Three years ago (it seems much longer) at a student body officer's convention in Boise, I met a girl whose father had recently been elected Governor of Idaho. I mention that fact because, had it not been the case, Bethy would never have come to Boise and we never would have met. I liked Bethy the first time we met. In fact, everybody liked Bethy. She was very different from most girls. She was a real pal and we treated her as such. Four of my best friends [Carl Burke, Stan Burns, Wade Fleetwood, and Bob Wardwell] took her in as one of the bunch. They all thought a great deal of Bethy though not so much as I did. We dated steadily, and the more I saw of her, the more deeply I felt about her. We had wonderful times together."

"Then college came along and, with it, the war. Bethy went off for Michigan, and I to Stanford. Since that time, I've seen Bethy only once. And I'd fallen for her... I know that now----I knew it then but things were too uncertain, and, well we were pretty young. That was more than a year ago. A great deal has happened in that time. Bethy says she thinks I've changed, and I have----so has she, perhaps. She may feel very differently when she sees me again. If things had gone along normally, I might have had a ring on her finger by now. But Schickelgruber [Adolph Hitler] changed all that. We might as well face the facts…. You know that a war means fighting. No one can predict what the outcome will be. It wouldn't be fair to Bethy to assume that all indefinite and well. Even if all this hell had not occurred, we would have had to have waited until we were both sure. As it is, I can do nothing more than tell her that I feel the same as always about her, and that if I've acted queerly, there are certain confounding reasons that I can't as yet explain. She's a champ, Art, every inch a woman, and knowing that, I only hope she'll understand.

Frosty.

The fall of a vital communications link in North Burma...will make it possible to link...the old Burma Road thus establishing a new military supply route from India to China.

N.Y. Times 8/5/1944

Camp Ritchie, MD
August 5, 1944

Dearest Bethine,

Now that the Army has closed in on me once again, it feels as if our visit together had just been a passing dream--- a little bit of fancy in a world of hard fact and dull routine. It lasted so little time, and passed so rapidly. I only wish I were with you now high up and hidden awing in the mountains of home.

My trip out was long and, for the most part, uneventful. ...

The next morning I met some of my fellow classmen in the Baltimore station so we made the trip to Ritchie together. I couldn't help but contrast our arrival with what it had been six months before. We had a staff car waiting for at the station. We were ushered to the Post Headquarters where the necessary administrative details were taken care of. After a satisfying meal at the officer's mess, were taken to our quarters located across the lake overlooking the club and parade ground. It is Sunday, and the canoes are out on the lake. Many are swimming. The bright colors of the swimming suits and summer dresses set against a background of trees and Maryland hills, give the whole scene a rather pleasant, non-military appearance. Only the barracks on the hillside beyond remind me that I am very much a part of the Army, and that hard work begins tomorrow.

That's the news of these last five days. I wanted to write at length of more serious things. But my mood, after having just returned to the Army is quite bad despite the new privileges and responsibilities. I didn't want this letter to sound morbid.

Write often and soon -----

My love, Frosty

Allied planes maintained their relentless pounding of Japanese bases and shipping in the Pacific...China has proposed to the United States and Great Britain an international police force...to maintain peace.

N.Y. Times 8/29/1944

Camp Ritchie, MD
29 August 1944

Dearest Bethy,

By now, Bethy, I must write and tell you as simply and honestly as I can how much it meant to me to be with you those few days at home. I only hope that you enjoyed them as much as I did.

With your sparkle and many charms, you are also a very sensitive girl. If you show affection and I don't seem to respond, don't think too badly of me for it. You see, I'm not built quite the same way although I feel just as deeply nonetheless. Then too, Bethy, if we had both broken down---and there was much good reason for it---the little happiness we did salvage might well have gone unredeemed.

Your letter was very cheerful—fresh like the early morning in the hills about the [Robinson] Bar [Ranch]. I surely hope the Bar was all we anticipated. Take in the mountain air, and have fun, and if you have the time, enjoy a little of it for me. Tell the folks that the chicken dinner was swell, and that the wallet Chase gave me is reserved exclusively for my dress uniform.

I hope our talk has cleared up many questions. I know the answers weren't pleasant nor the immediate prospects reassuring. It would have been much easier, much safer in many ways, to have kept the issues clouded, but it wouldn't have been right nor fair to you. God knows I hated to admit the answers, even to myself. I hope that they will work out, and I've reason to expect that they will. But until they do, they leer up to torment me, to twist and war my plans and happiness.

You are normal and mature, Bethy. You needn't complicate your life with an emptiness of any kind. I won't take the chance of ruining it for you. That's why we must wait. That's why you must go back to Michigan and give yourself every chance to know and love another. You must be sure, Bethy. And if you find another, even if he's a West Pointer, I'll be throwing rice at the wedding for your sake. If you don't, then we'll have to wait and hope and pray that all your stories—even your own—have happy endings.

My love to you,

Frosty

American forces gave emphatic warning to Japan that they were getting ready to reclaim the Philippines.

N.Y. Times, 9/16/1944

Camp Ritchie, MD
Near the Pennsylvania border
September 16, 1944

Dearest Bethine,

I hope that I haven't revealed any military information that might locate Camp Ritchie as a potential target for German robot bombs. In a desperate effort to wreck the very "nerve center" of this war, the Nazis might launch these weird weapons from submarines in Chesapeake Bay. At least that would stir things up a bit. I might even see some action!

Speaking of action, Washington beckoned last week and I answered in the form of a visit... An officer in my group drove two of us into the city, and we agreed to meet at the Statler [Hotel] at ten o'clock Monday morning for the return trip Monday morning rolled around all too quickly. The two of us waited in the lobby all morning but neither the car nor the drive appeared. About noon an M.P. phoned to tell us that ... was at Walter Reed Hospital. We learned from him an hour later that some wave had pushed him out of a second story window. Don't ask me what was going on. These Washington women must be getting mighty rugged. They must be out to prove that there is something to this song, "The WACS and the WAVES Will Win the War."

Now look here, McGee. If you keep jumping at wrong conclusions, I'll talk myself right out of a sweet-heart. You don't take my soul-searching, heart-felt letters the right way. You misinterpret them. You seek a hidden meaning in what I do say, and then write me back what you think I don't, Bethy. I'm too sincere--- or anyway to simple---to be subtle. If I had ever wanted to say to you, "Go-on I just [have] no place for you in my life," I would have said it with vigor. Forget my last letter if you can. I had no right to expect that you could understand it. I must have been feeling sorry for myself.

Bob [Wardwell] hasn't written. My letter must not have reached him. Just received a long discourse on marriage from the new-born authority, Eldred… "Marriages are built on such wonderful things as a complete companionship and a closeness so intense that one often mistakes even his own identity with that of his wife." He then warms up to more intimate subjects… You can imagine, Bethy, what a masterpiece it is. Oh, oh! ! !.

I am spending fifteen minutes each day "taking it easy and relaxing." I expect quite an improvement soon. May I think of you when I relax?

My love,

Frosty

> *One Enemy Drive Checked in China...Troops of the southern wing of the double-barreled Japanese offensive into southeastern China have driven deeper...the Chinese High Command reported...*
>
> N.Y. Times 10/12/1944

```
                                    Camp Ritchie, MD
                                    October 12, 1944
```

Dear Bethy,

Mother has probably told you of the manifold difficulties on the trip east. The uncertainties of arriving late coupled with the gloom of returning to the Army left me somewhat tense. Your letter served to help me begin to relax again. In that respect at least, I am improving by the day.

Aside from the routine preparations underway here at camp, the only news I have concerns a couple of trips to Washington. Both were delightful in every way. Last Sunday we motored down to Mt. Vernon (We had planned to go by boat, but the crew were on strike). It was warm, bright, and cheerful; flowers were still in bloom, and the blue waters of the Potomac reflected grandly the multi-colored finale of the dying leaves. Washington rests as he once lived, in sheltered and simply dignity.

That evening we dined in the gardens of a colonial restaurant in Alexandria. We did so in Mother's honor-the name "Laura"

[Laura Bilderback Church] being that of the restaurant. And it was truly a good omen for the meal proved to be excellent.

Perhaps you have seen Christ Church in Alexandria. If not, it's a lovely old church attended in their time by both Washington and Lee. We took our turn---much as little children might do---sitting in the pew of each, and noticed with surprise, two silver plaques on the back of Washington's seat commemorating the visit of Roosevelt and Churchill in 1942. The good general must have turned in his grave!

I was in the city again yesterday afternoon. While there, I found time to see the picture, "Arsenic and Old Lace." If you haven't seen the play, Bethy, by all means see the show. It is wonderful.

That my leaving had no effect on your appetite, was a serious disappointment. I had hoped that some kind of diet, preferably one involuntarily applied, would come to rescue you and your waistline. Betty lay off the sweets.

I have no idea how long I'll be here at Ritchie. However, I'll keep writing and keep my address posted correctly so that your letters will reach me uninterrupted. In the meantime, don't forget to write as often as you can.

With love to you,

Frosty

"Burma Road Point is Won by Chinese;...British Occupy...in the Drive Toward Mandalay."

N.Y. Times 1/4/1945

Frank Church in a rickshaw in Shanghai, China, 1945.

Shanghai [China]
4 January 1945

Dearest Bethy,

Writing on a pencil pad has the advantage of helping to make my script more legible and at the same time enables me to write on straight lines. Besides, it represents the only paper available at the moment.

This morning we are suffering the confusion of another reorganization. We have just moved into larger offices, this being a typical "consolidation" effort which results, rather than in a curtailment of strength, in an increase of work requiring an increase of personnel. The "Mess and Billeting" office has been elevated to the status of the "Office of the Headquarters Commandant," and I have been transferred from mess to supply. But this again may be only temporary. For more than a month now there have been requests from Theater G-2 for orders transferring me back to the fold, and since the quest for "bodies" goes on endlessly, I may end up there yet.

The holiday season was festive and colorful here in Shanghai. The… made every effort to entertain Earl, Dave and me in a very generous way. We spent Christmas Eve with them in their apartment, sharing a candle-lit tree, exchanging gifts, singing Christmas carols, discussing the different yuletide customs we separately honored, listening to Brahms and Beethoven, and feasting upon the traditional German goose, cooked apples, and fine Rhine wine. On Christmas morning we all motored into the country to a [?} given by a mutual friend... an old China hand, a rather well-known artist, and a very interesting guy.

Christmas was pleasant---I felt detached from the Army among gracious, stimulating people, with friends met socially once again. Our Christmas was quiet and cheerful, and as satisfying as I could possibly hope for apart from home.

New Years, however, we greeted in a very different spirit. Again the...were hosts, and the party was boisterous and happily extravagant. We dined and danced in the 14th floor sky room gardens of the fashionable Park Hotel, affirming our hopes for the coming year with toasts of sparkling champagne. We laughed and had fun, forgetting for the night—or nearly so---the estrangement and uncertainty shrouding the weeks and months ahead.

Bethy, I feel terribly bad about the expectations you and the folks held out for my momentary arrival at home. Of course, I should have realized that with the return of so many, with the misleading press releases, and with my own premature optimism at a time when the avowed program was that of deactivating the theater, that you probably would expect no other. But it has now become evident that a considerable body of American troops will remain in China on a semi-permanent basis. The number, having been reduced to about 10,000 is now actually going to be increased again through the procurement of low-point inductees from the States. Officers who are now in China will be released only as they become eligible for discharge on points, or on length of service. Since I have only 56 points and just less than three years' service, the point requirement now being 70 and the service four years, you can see, Bethy, that I'll be ineligible for redeployment for some time to come. It's not pleasant to contemplate, but perhaps I really have no legitimate protest. I was most fortunate during the war to have been in China, relatively safe and comfortable. My work and associations, together with many singular experiences, were on a level very few others had the chance to know. Now the payment comes, and it comes in the form of additional service overseas. Still, it's not easy to reconcile myself to it when I can see so little justification for the policy.

Bert…was here this afternoon (I began this letter earlier, and have been returning to it at odd-moments through the day). He is on his way home for medical reasons, and expects to be in Boise within the month. I'm not sure that you remember… but at any note he remembers you very well---which is not surprising---and I've asked him to be sure to contact you if possible.

Bethy, I hope your Christmas was merry and your new year as happy for you as for those who, being with you, were bound to find it.

My love,

Frosty

"The Battle for Iwo…Volcano Island's Defenses are Probably Strongest ….of Any Ground

In the World…N.Y. Times 3/5/1945

At Sea
5 March 1945

Dear Bethy,

Today was bright and hot. Since early morning, the sun has burned down with an intensity that even the steaming deserts near Glenns Ferry seldom suffer. Still, it was a welcome relief! My spirits seem to rise and fall with the weather. For a full week now, the skies, low and overcast, have turned the ocean an unfriendly gray. I felt the gloom of the sober, melancholy sky. But this evening a copper moon dominates the star-studded heavens, striking a luminous path across an unruffled sea.

We are told that these waters are particularly dangerous. (It is a "100%" zone which means that the merchant crewmen aboard get double pay!). A reinforced watch is posted, the guns are cocked and loaded, and the ship zig-zags crazily. I find it hard to believe, on so beautiful a night that enemy submarines hide beneath these quiet waters awaiting their prey in hopes for a sudden kill. The whole of the universe----with all of its magnificence, cold and barren----seems to look down and mock our puny impudence, our senseless savagery. On nights like these the war seems distant and unreal.

After you read my last letter, Bethy, you will have every right to question my fleeting sanity. Of course, I must own to its absurdity. There is an explanation, however, although a very feeble one. You see, Bethy, I was once told that the secret to good descriptive writing could be condensed into one easy rule: Write, don't think! Put down anything and everything that first occurs to you. Write of trivia. Don't sit before a typewriter and stare blankly at the empty paper. Don't ponder over the sentences, weighing this word against that. Write, don't think!

That was the advice of a friend of mine who possesses unquestionable literary abilities. Having understandable respect for his opinions, I set out to apply his rule. I did so with the intention of painting for you an eloquent picture of ocean and sky. And look what happened! Why in thirty short minutes I revealed, I foolishly exposed the whole blatant confusion of my mental processes! And then, Bethy, did I destroy the evidence? Did I quietly tear the sheets into shreds and set a match to them? Oh no! Thinking the letter to be funny, I quickly sealed the envelope, and sent the letter to you.

You will be interested to know that I received a long letter from Carl shortly before leaving the United States. He was badly discouraged, almost bitter. And for that I can't blame him. After three months of action on the Western front, he was made a PfC! He certainly has suffered from a host of rotten breaks. He swallowed his pride to blame himself for our misunderstanding, and to ask that we become good friends again. That's more than I would have done. I couldn't help but feel that he is sincere. Two years of silence constitutes convincing evidence that we both share at least one common characteristic, stubbornness. We were always friends. We might even become good friends again, but I doubt that we ought to make another attempt at being the best of friends. [In fact, they became best friends for life]. Does that sound selfish? Does it testify to my vindictiveness? I hope not, for I bear no grudges. What do you think, Bethy?

I've been awfully fortunate in getting two splendid men on my team. They are both young, although older than yours truly. From the physical standpoint, they are both very tall and slender. Together, we look like the best part of a forgotten basketball team. The tech. sergeant, Bill…hails from Atlanta, Georgia. He possesses a natural charm both in manner and speech, enhanced by a colorful Southern accent. He's alert, active, often eloquent, and always witty. Nathaniel…the staff sergeant and third member of our trio, comes from the best Philadelphian society. His father is an influential lawyer there; his family of old Republican stock, has long been prominent in Pennsylvanian politics. In fact, his grandfather was governor of the State during the period of Teddy Roosevelt's reign in the White House. [he] interests me even more… and I should like to have him for a good friend. There's the rub! Although our unit is so small that the familiar Army barriers break down, my relationship to the two is and remains, nonetheless, that of employer-employee where, however thoughtful and considerate the employer, however "pro-labor" his sentiments, however friendly he may be toward those he hires, he does not and cannot share the comradeship they feel toward one another. Bill and Penny are bed-follows, so to speak, in a small unit, a tiny apartment in which I must occupy the adjoining room. We don't stand on common ground. We can't deal with one another man to man.

Bethy, when I write next I shall be able to put "Somewhere in…" on the letterhead. Even though I have not yet arrived, I feel lonely and depressed. I hope you will write often. Your letters are always a comfort, and I look forward to receiving them with an anxious anticipation. I'm not good at expressing my feelings, so, for the most part, they go unexpressed. But do write, Bethy, and remember that you are always in my thoughts.

Good night and love,

Frosty

"India Greets U.S. Editors...Okinawa Glitters As Military Prize...A double blow as any military defeat...has been inflicted on Japan by Moscow's curt denunciation of the Russo-Japanese neutrality pact..."

N.Y. Times 4/6/1945.

New Delhi, India

6 April 1945

Dearest Bethy,

Late yesterday afternoon I was handed a neatly bound bundle of mail. There were twenty-six letters in all. Six were from you. It had been more than nine weeks since I had received a letter of any kind. I hurried back to my quarters, set a chair before the fireplace, ordered a cold drink, and leaned back to hungrily absorb all the news from home.

I arranged your letters in chronological order, as best I could, and opened the first, dated early in January. When I finished reading it, I felt as if I had just been wrung through a ringer, and had fallen loosely into a bucket of limp wash. I felt like hiding in some dark corner, just to whimper and lick the wounds. That would have been less manly, but a hell of a lot easier than trying to defend myself! You challenged me for an answer, and I have none. You told me that I had, in effect been callous and rotten, and I had been. You have a right to a full and honest explanation, an explanation I'm at a loss to provide. Bethy, I don't mean to hurt you. I'd do anything to make you happy. Inconsiderate I am in every way, but that's too gentle a word. Only a selfish, thick-headed good-for-nothing would act as I have acted. I qualify for a dunce's booby prize. Still, self-denunciation, however justified, doesn't help. To say that I'm sorry is helplessly weak and empty. I'm just guilty, that's all, and you ought to stick the knife in deep, and turn it around and around.

But I didn't come to Michigan for a "cheap good time." And what I found wasn't cheap. You should know that. I did have a "grand time" and you made it grand, and I wanted to thank you, to thank you sincerely. If I were looking for common pleasures, I could find them easily enough. And I would find them elsewhere---not in Michigan. You should know that too!!

Well, Bethy, for the first time in many weeks I can pin-point my location. My new address is on the envelope. If you use it from now on it will avoid unnecessary delays.

New Delhi, as you probably know, is the capital of India. Is so strikingly different from the rest of the country that you feel the sharp contrast between Western and Eastern civilizations here as nowhere else in India. Delhi is English---that is New Delhi --- relatively clean, expansive, and modern. Yet, the city is so new, the buildings so much alike, being all finished in cream stucco and built in the plain, functional style, that it actually gives the appearance of being a housing project, done on an ambitious scale. Only the "tongas," the ox carts, and the Indian costumes, are traces of the real India without.

My own quarters are unbelievably fine. I share a room of palatial size with another lieutenant. We are equipped with a private shower and bath, a fireplace if you please, two bureaus, a desk, a ceiling fan, two spacious closets, a magazine table that sits squarely in the middle of the room, and two easy chairs that sit on either side of the table. We have rented a radio, for the Army stations broadcast our regular national programs about a week late, and an ice box that the "bearer" keeps stocked with coke and cold beer.

Yes, Bethy, I said "bearer." You see, it's the custom here to hire an Indian servant to take charge of the household duties. So I find myself, the champion (so I like to think!) of the down-trodden, with a personal servant. Al Hadad is most efficient. A handkerchief, neatly folded, lays on the bureau, keys, pencils, and the like are always transferred to my clean uniform, and my shoes are polished twice daily. Al Hadad insisted at first on helping me dress, but that was really carrying things too far. As long as I'm here in Delhi—and it's likely to be temporarily—I can't say that I'm suffering the hardships of war. You can quit worrying, if you worry, Bethy, and you can write Mother to take down the service flag in the window, at least for some weeks to come.

Although I have only been in India a couple of weeks, I've seen much of it. There are some obvious observations. The people are incredibly poor. They crowd together in filthy hovels, often built of mud, and filled with flies and smoke from the open fires. The stench is often unbearable. I am fast becoming very much attached to the "sacred cows." Of all of India's unfortunates, they are the healthiest, and probably the cleanest. You are likely to encounter a cow most anywhere and, of course, it is a serious offense not to treat her respectfully. Luckily, I'm situated on the second floor, so I'm not likely to suffer from a bed partner!

A week ago, on the last night of a long trek across India, the three of us made our pilgrimage to the Taj Mahal. The Taj is fully as fabulous as its reputation. It defies description. We were fortunate enough to see it by the light of the full moon and, resting as it did in the early evening mist, it looked like a heavenly vision. So gracefully are the straight lines and arches blended, so grand is it simplicity, so perfectly balanced it proportions, that even closely, it looks impossibly unreal. The effect of the Taj Mahal is one of incomparable majesty.

Well, Bethy, there's much more to tell you, but I shall write again soon. My roommate is trying to sleep without success, for this is not a noiseless typewriter. It's late and I am tired---as you can judge from the numerous mistakes in typing—so for now,

Love, Frosty

p.s. Your letter with your senior picture enclosed arrived late this afternoon. I shall put the picture in my wallet where it will fit very nicely. Thanks very much. I needed a good picture of you badly.

"Last Stand in East Ordered by Hitler…Big Gain in Burma… The stage was rapidly being set in Burma…that will end with the final expulsion of the Japanese armies…

N.Y. Times 4/17/1945

APO N.Y.C.
17 April 1945

Dearest Bethy,

This is just a v-mail note and is not to be considered, in any way, as an honest letter.

I can say, I suppose, that I'm no longer stationed at that paradise I spoke of in my last letter. A deal like that is really too good to last. Those people just look at me in complete bewilderment, rush into inference, and then move me on my way again. I really expected them to fight over my talents! When I'm settled again, you can expect a long letter. Sent you a package from India. Hope it arrives in good shape.

Love, Frosty

"Good Faith Pledged Parley Opening...the four sponsoring powers of the United Nations Conference gave public assurance...of their good faith and unrelenting efforts...to chart a new organization for world security."

N.Y. Times 4/17/1945

April 27, 1945

Dearest Frosty,

I just got your first letter and your package! Also, I fully realize that I'm in such a marvelous mood that this might turn into a letter with which I could be blackmailed.

Didn't you read any [illegible] never have written a letter telling you just how I felt like that.

Maybe someday I'll calm down and not fly off the handle one way or the other—but it's doubtful and not a promise. It almost seems like it would be boring not to feel strongly one way or another now and then.

I'm happy anything can burst the bubble but at this moment it's complete. My happiness is quite commonplace, and I can't give you the thrill of getting a letter and a purse from New Delhi, India, but here goes anyway. For two weeks this place for me has been chaos and confusion, little sleep, little time to eat, etc. I see Marty at noon or asleep in bed when I come in. But, finally an address from Frosty.

My statue cast and turned out with no air bubbles on the nose, etc.--1,200 tickets sold to Gene Krupa, the first time the co-eds have swung a big name dance. I'm wearing my old pink satin formal which Mom revised by cutting out the sleeves, and I bought black gloves (long above my elbows); and a black purse with gold on it came from India to match the gloves and gold earrings. Oh! Frosty, it was all sort of a thrown together outfit, but you'd think it had been planned.... said it looked smooth—bless her. I needed it. My hair was full of plaster from the casting; we still had 50 more tickets to sell and the program's hadn't arrived yet (this was yesterday).

Then from Mom's and Helen, P.E.O chapter came an invitation to join. Mom hadn't been at the last meeting, she wrote, and Helen gave quite a plug for me. She certainly has been a wonderful friend.

Frosty, write whenever you can. I haven't waited for answering letters for a long time…now don't you.

I loved your description of Delhi, and you with a "bearer" and of course, you big lug, I worry and was awfully relieved just to know you hadn't joined the Navy. You see the two letters I'd had were both at sea!

Your letters sound a great deal like… brother; he's in India and has been to New Delhi.

Frosty, I'm green with envy. I want to travel and to see the Taj Mahal in the moonlight. I'll stow away if you'll show it to me. Or, heavens, is that being presumptuous? I'll promise only to look at it as a wonder with the awe, knowledge and admiration of a scholar and a student! Ahem!??

This has got to find its way into an envelope, and me down to lunch. It's wonderful to know where you are. It is a beautiful purse—thank you---and all the girls say you have marvelous taste.

I agree and send love,

Bethy

"Burma Japanese Pursued; Allied Land Forces Meet Firm Resistance."

N.Y. Times 5/13/1945

13 May 1945
Kunming, China

Dearest Bethine,

As you can see from the letterhead, Bethy, my leisurely life in New Delhi came to a sudden end even before I had a fair chance to relax. I came to China across the fabulous Lido-Burma Road and, as much of it punishes a provincial like myself to admit it, I have never before seen such spectacular country. Nature carved out China on a wild and lavish scale. All along the road, high above the tiny valleys and wind-swept plateaus, the barren mountains rise in stern magnificence. And the road winds its way over, around, and across these low Himalayas for a thousand miles into China.

In many ways I'm glad to have come to China. It's much cooler here. The Chinese are friendlier than the Indians and, although fully as poor, they appear to be cleaner and more industrious. Nowhere is this more apparent than in their farming. The Chinese didn't have to be taught either the value of irrigation dangers of erosion. Where the stream bed interferes, a hollowed bamboo log serves as a primitive aqueduct. Rice, of course, is the staple crop, and in no other way can it be grown. The result, however, is that the land-pressed Chinese are able to farm the steepest mountain sides up to altitudes of seven and eight thousand feet.

I wish you could have seen the children along the road. When we stopped to eat, great swarms of them would cluster about to beg for food. The little two-year olds carry the one-year olds on their backs, and the tiny babies, just big enough to hold on, stretch out a bitty fist with thumb upraised to give "thumbs up" and shout their "Ding How" greeting. They would grab up our offerings greedily, and carry our empty cartons away.

News of the President's [Franklin Roosevelt] death [April 12, 1945] struck the Orient with ominous misgiving. I was in New Delhi at the time. The British flags, as well as the Chinese here, were lowered in tribute. Even the waiters, whom I had supposed to be totally hostile and indifferent, asked anxiously about him. I suppose that Franklin Roosevelt was held in higher esteem by more ordinary people all over the world than any other living figure. His successor, God pity him, faces an incredible challenge, but he seems to be taking over with a firm hand.

Bethy, if in weak moments of folly, you ever chance to worry about us, stop right now! I'm settled now doing the work I was trained to do. At present I'm well out of range of the Japanese, and, even should the situation change, I'm too thin to be hit anyway. The work I do is important work, absorbing work, and my associates are splendid fellows. As a result, the general atmosphere is as pleasant as could be hoped for.

Right now my desk is stacked high with unfinished work beckoning me away from the typewriter. But first, let me tell you that your letters have been arriving regularly. They are wonderful letters, especially the last, and I intend to answer them topic by topic as soon as I catch up and get back on my feet again. So for now, this must do. It will serve to give you a synopsis of my whereabouts and doings, and I hope it will convey to you my appreciation for the way you've written. Your letters always mean an awful lot.

My friend Gene is now in San Francisco as a member of the American delegation at the [United Nations] conference. Bob

Wardwell writes that you're still his favorite person---as you are mine---and he enclosed a picture of himself in the cockpit of his plane. Now that the European war has ended, it's a great relief to know that my friends over there are safe. With our full attention directed against Japan, the war in the Pacific may not last so long. Perhaps you have heard that…l was wounded some time ago. If not, rest easy for he's well on his way toward recovery. Wade Fleetwood is now at the University of Idaho, and that's about all the news I can think of. Carl wrote a second letter immediately after receiving my reply. We seem to be on good terms again. What a comedy!

Send us a picture of your "clay man" when he's ready for his debut. I need something to cover up the picture you sent of yourself! It's with this note of sweet sentimentality that I must draw my ravings to a close.

Love always, Frosty

p.s. I surely hope that the prom turns out to be a great success. I'm sure it did. McGee, when you put on a party, you put on a party!!

"Cutbacks in airplane production, eliminating 17,000 planes scheduled for the next eighteen months, were announced by the War Department."

N.Y. Times 5/26/1945

Dear Bethy … Dear Frosty …

Bethine Church's sculpture at the University of Michigan

26 May 1945
Kunming, China

Dear Bethy,

You are now looked upon by those of the section with that degree of suitable respect men of all ages render to young women they consider talented. And I, ever your staunch supporter, carefully guard the hidden truth. So expertly has the matter been handled, and so remote are the possibilities of actual acquaintance in the future, that even the most prying, the most skeptical, freely concede that I have an artist for a girl-friend. Seriously, Bethy, your "Modesty" took the office by storm. We all agree, and there is among us a sculptor of no mean talent, that your contribution to the Annual Exhibition stood head and shoulders---an I speak figuratively—above all the others shown. Our collective congratulations!

I'm very happy, but not surprised, that your dance turned out so well. Wouldn't it have been great if we could have gone together? I often recall the wonderful time we had in Detroit last December. Here's to more and better times after the war.

What am I going to do with a college graduate on my hands! Do you think I can manage with the qualms of an inferiority complex? When I think about the long years of college still ahead of me, the prospect of a tottering, long-bearded, old man clutching his coveted parchment, looms up to trouble my sleep. What about your plans regarding Mexico? If you go through with it, we might plan on a reunion in Mexico City. Let me hear from you on the subject.

This letter is only of post-card length, but I hope it will serve to let you know that I intend to write much more frequently, if only at times briefly, for you are always in my thoughts. That long treatise I promised is still in the offing, but it will come as soon as the pressure of our work here lifts to give us a short respite. In the meantime, please keep writing regularly. You should know how much your letters mean to me.

I have included in the envelope a Chinese bill. It may be of some interest if you haven't seen one before. China is caught up in the chaos of uncontrolled inflation. The unofficial rate of exchange now varies between seven and eight hundred to one. More next time.

My best love,

Frosty

"Marines Win Base...Troops Gain Despite Mud...Tactical Planes Now Using New Fields Against Japan...Tokyo Calls Japan Fortress of Caves..."

N.Y. Times 6/7/1945

7 June 1945
Kunming, China

Dear Bethy,

For fully five minutes I sat here at the desk considering the advisability of writing this letter, as by all rights it should be written, with pen and ink. My pen just arrived, and if not other letter is written manually, those to you certainly ought to be. But here were two, just two factors weighing against it. First of all, I can say more before exhaustion when using a typewriter. Secondly, and more significantly, I have only green ink in my pen. Thus I run the risk of letting you know how green with envy it makes as when I think about the lucky characters at Michigan and elsewhere who can, by virtue of location alone, date you at your pleasure. Blue ink might have been exchanged, but then the whole situation makes me just as "blue" as it does envious, so you see there was no escaping the typewriter!

I had intended to send you something for a graduation present. However, so far I've seen nothing half-way presentable here in Kunming. Other officers, who have been here for some time and know the ropes, mysteriously turn up with attractive gifts from time to time so that I haven't as yet given up hope. They tell us that one has to find pretty Oriental girls who know their way around.

My first encounter with a comparatively large group of young Chinese came about the other day when one of the officers in the section, who was scheduled to lead a discussion for a class of interpreters, asked me to take his place. I had a thoroughly enjoyable time. All of those in the group, although they had studied English in the universities and understood if fairly well, had never before spoken with an American. Some were frightened. All looked upon an American with mixed feelings. But after the ice was broken, they began to show interest and spirit. My capacity of diplomacy was put to a severe test when several asked at once "Why should the British be allowed to take back Hong Kong?" Now there, Bethy, is a good question! Answering it to everybody's satisfaction without saying anything---for there was nothing to say---was a ticklish proposition. Then somebody wanted to know what were the customs of the American people, and I discovered, after having spent all my life in the United States, nothing quite so difficult as describing the customs of the American people. We moved on without success to another question. It was a honey! A little man got up from the back of the room to ask, "What do you think should be the prerequisite to a lasting peace?" Second Lieutenants aren't even supposed to think about the prerequisites for a lasting peace, let alone discuss them with the Chinese. But I was soundly trapped, finally managing to garble out something that seemed to correspond to their own feelings. They were enthusiastic in the agreement, and I now have an invitation for a return engagement.

Bethy, you and I have to have a genuine Chinese dinner when we are together again. The Chinese are among the world's finest cooks. We will eat, at your permission or, for that matter, without it, with chop sticks, and we will order neither noodles nor chop suey, but real Chinese food. Although the inflation makes eating out expensive, the excellence of the food tempts us into Kunming for regular weekly feasts. It is in this connection that we have spent several pleasant, informative evenings with a small group of British officers. The nature of the work here brings us into contact with these gentlemen---the word being used in its most "correct" sense---and that contact has in turn necessitated a social acquaintanceship, which in its turn had led to several interesting get-togethers. It's all very complicated. In fact, I seem to be repeating myself. Anyway, you get the idea.

Do you remember Bert…? Certainly not as well as he remembers you. He called me up a few days ago to tell me he was in Kunming, which was obvious enough anyway, and to invite us to take him out to dinner. It as a … dollar dinner, but old talk of old times made it worth the price. Idaho men are scattered thinly in the service, so that when two Boise men meet up with one another in Kunming, China, it's really cause for celebration.

Have I mentioned before that my good friend Gene… is one of the American delegation at the San Francisco Conference? If not, I'll gloat about it now. Bob…wrote recently to tell us that he had completed his 40th mission, meaning that he might get back to the States in a few months. I sure hope so.

Bethy, keep on writing regularly, will you? I hope my letters are coming through more often for I intend to keep writing more often from now on. I miss you lots, Bethy, and your letters mean the world to me.

Until next time-----

My love,

Frosty

p.s. This is to show that I really do have green ink in the pen, that I haven't completely lost my ability to write, and that I think you will be "queen" of the class at Michigan or anywhere---wherever you go.

"Might-Have-Beens in War...previously withheld stories of what might have happened if critical events had turned just a hairbreadth more in Germany's favor."

N.Y. Times 6/10/1945

June 10, 1945

Dear Frosty,

I know what a terrible letter I wrote last week. Funny but it reflected my whole feeling. Ann Arbor and everything that was happening was so much with me that nothing else seemed reality. You've never seemed so far away. There was nothing but this small air-tight world and the world and people in it. Then you came through with that wonderful letter. Thank you, sir, for your support and those around you for the idea that I even come near being a sculptor. But, that wasn't the best. You must have been in a quite mellow mood down the typical "Frosty" last paragraph on inflation. Funny, I've been so well trained not to think in terms of "we" that your references to reunion in Mexico City, etc. quite took me off my feet. But, then, I remembered the warm climate and realized how those things happen. Quite seriously, however, it was a sweet and wonderful letter and a nice one to study for finals on.

I had planned to go to Mexico City, but if I go "Red Cross," it will be changed (wonder if they'd give the China theater of operations). Wish I could this minute talk to you a few minutes. Do you think it's a good idea? Do you like it for me? I pride

Dear Bethy ... Dear Frosty ...

myself a bit in the fact that you would have something to say on whether you'd think it a good idea and that frankly.

Tomorrow begins my last week of classes, then finals—the folks will be out.

The West Point scourge has gone, and I think I still remained heart free and fancy flying.

Harriet and I just went out for some soup. The night doesn't seem quite right for it—it's the warmest yet. The sky tonight is beautiful with violet and pink-salmon clouds. Tomorrow, when we buckle down for the last grind, will no doubt be a beautiful day.

I saw a movie "Objective Burma" today, and though I believe you in saying your o.k., if anything does get tight, don't forget to turn sidewise.

Now, to crack the unworn books and make them think they've been read.

After next week there may be new things popping so off I go. Thank you for keeping the answers to a few of these crazy letters in mind. I shall be looking forward to the treatise.

With love,

Bethy

"Longhand note of President Harry Truman:

At the meeting of June 18, 1945, the invasion plan for Japan was discussed. General Marshall's plan was approved."

N.Y. Times 6/18/1945

```
                                           18 June 1945
                                          Kunming, China
```

Dearest Bethy,

Nothing in China ever works very well. "Made In China" is the trademark of inferiority. The first day we moved into our new headquarters, the windows wouldn't open, and when forced open, wouldn't shut. When we forced them shut, the hinges fell off, and the carpenters had to be called for. It was a bad day all around. We tried to work amid a wild infusion of noises. Hammering, and sawing, and pounding! Finally, late in the afternoon, we left the office, but found out that the door, which had been standing open all day, refused to shut. So, we forced it shut and---you guessed it---the door knob came off! Nothing in China ever works very well.

Bethy, I can appreciate the way you feel about "doing your part." Coming overseas has its attraction, and I'd give anything if we could be together. Even if there were a chance of that—and the possibility is very remote---I would advise against it. Men out here, to put it bluntly, hungry for women. Inhibitions that they would otherwise foster are thrown to the wind. You can understand that, Bethy, and I imagine my mention of it constitutes no startling revelation. I have no doubts about you, Bethy. You could go anywhere and defy the worst. But many haven't, and although full credit should go to the Red Cross girls, I've seen in [illegible] for the wonderful work they've done, the association all in all is not the best. In fact, it's downright rotten! I can see you now saying "What does he think I am anyway, a waterlily? It's not that, Bethy, and of course it's up to you to decide. I just think your heart ought to "murmur" against it. At least, mine does!

About a week ago, a friend and I commandeered a jeep for a Sunday afternoon trip to West Mountains. We were out to see the Chinese temples situated high above Lake Kunming. But our trip was badly timed. We had no sooner begun the uncertain drive toward the third set of temples when the sun suddenly slipped behind the mountains across the valley. It grew rapidly dark, while the road we were attempting to negotiate narrowed and roughened until it more closely resembled a pony trail. Finally we were forced to a stop and found ourselves precariously balanced on a six foot ledge some twelve hundred feet above the lake. I'm convinced I'm convinced that if either of us had jumped, we would have bounced just twice before striking the water. It took us nearly an hour to cautiously back the jeep down the trail for half a mile before finding room to turn around. The evening had been an adventuresome one, but drama was added in the course of our retreat when the melancholy temple gongs began to sound. We were afraid that we had invaded the sacred sanctuary, making great haste to retire. I wish you might have been along.

A dollar an hour! It just goes to prove you have real talent, Bethy. How is the clay man doing? No better I hope than the West Pointer!

The lights are going out---even the electricity refuses to function in China—so I must close.

Keep the letters coming.

Much love, Frosty

"U.S Ships Hit Foe at Sea...Japanese forces...withdrawing from Chinas 'rice bowl'...under attacks by American fighter pilots...

N.Y. Times 6/28/1945

Thursday, June 28, 1945

Dearest Frosty,

I haven't your letter here to answer. I got it the first final exam. Isn't it strange two years ago I got your wings just before a final letter and my morale certainly was at low ebb. It also was very sweet of you to think of getting me something but don't worry about it. I can certainly imagine how the service one have [illegible] the country—it's the thought that counts. By the by I had a funny experience in Detroit last night. John and Muriel had taken us all out to dinner (Pop, Mom and Beulah) and we stopped in a Vernon's place for some ginger ale, when suddenly... beckoned me over to a (and I'm not exaggerating) tall blond Air Corps. Lt. who asked me if the bag I was carrying wasn't from the shop in New Delhi. His mother had gotten one from his brother. Gee whiz, and if I hadn't been leaving his morning, just think of what an introduction your purse would have made for me! (tongue in cheek). No fooling though it is beautiful, and I carry it with even short dinner dresses in the evening, and people always comment!

By the by the waiting is strictly a product of the train. We are on our way to Chicago. We're staying at the Palmer House tonight then off to Idaho tomorrow (we hope—reservations are scarce as hen's teeth). At the first of the month they are probably going to close civilian travel; it's probably a good idea, but we are in a way essential---Beulah,--Pops brought to take through the University clinic. She has been having some rather serious trouble. We hope now have a good diagnosis and that they can help her.

We stopped at the…and also Muriel and John's. David asked where was the "so-so." I haven't meant to neglect writing but we certainly have when being entertained. I do hope you can read this.

Between semesters Pops and Mom (in lieu of the car which will wait until after the war) gave me a lovely diamond ring (you know Pops) and when they came out they bought the sweetest amethyst pin to match my earrings a year ago. Really it's been quite a graduation. Now, to work heavens. I certainly am swinging in mid-air after all my previous definite plans. I certainly wish I could get your view on the Red Cross---some say yes, some no.

Your experience with the Chinese sounds like something you'd like to do in China as a civilian. As to Chinese food, I do enjoy it, but young man, just because you're a Lt. and used to group command, does that mean you can make the statement you made about chop sticks—whether or no. Well anyway I've been able to eat with chop sticks since Pop was in the Legislature, and I was nine. A lady who'd spent a great deal of time in China taught me! So there.

Of course, I remember Bert. I'm awfully glad to hear you got together, though your dinner sounded quite expensive. It was nice that he remembered me (though you didn't say in what way!).

You see I feel just as good as you did when you wrote your last letter. Lt., what makes you think they take me out right-by-place only. I'll send you the "Egoist" by Meredith. I do hope you realize at this point I'm kidding for actually, like the German line under the bomb crater (calling it a mouse hole) I feel that China is an awfully long way to be facetious. It's too hard to explain in case the crack goes astray.

I was however amazed that you should even think of turning "green" and as for that making you "blue" I've been under the impression that I was working under your instructions, and it was the least of your worries.

Gene…will probably have a great deal to say about the conference, though I'll bet his situation will be a bit like yours with the Chinese (tied up as to saying much of anything).

I have no doubt missed much in your letter. I shall look when I get it out of the trunk. If all goes well we'll be home Sunday, and I'll write the first of the week. Also, during the afternoon Mom and I got trimmed at bridge. But, we'll get them between Chicago and Omaha. You just watch those Oriental girls.

Love, Bethy

"They're Coming Back from the Pacific, Too; For many veterans the Japanese war in over."

N.Y. Times 7/8/1945

8 July 1945
Kunming, China

Dear Bethy,

As I write this evening, my spirits are affected by the humid oppressiveness that everywhere pervades the approaching darkness. It is a sober, melancholy evening. The sharp crack of thunder and the whining pools of wind give fare warning of the coming storm. For the summer months are here, and in China that means gray days under an ever-threatening sky. I can safely say, although not without the implication of levity, that nothing is more dampening to my contentment than rain. And the rains come to China in generous measure. Soon the paths are mud, and the roads are mud, and everything is wet to the touch. The omnipresent dreariness on the outside is turned to downright provocation on the inside by the inescapable fact that no roof in all of China will satisfactorily contain water. At first, the rain will penetrate with modest reluctance, the water falling in tiny droplets from the still resisting ceiling. The roof-tops fight in often valiant, but seldom determined, and never successful. Soon the water is pouring through in steady streams. Adroitly and with the ready skill resultant of both necessity and experience, we move the beds beneath the interval of space that can be sometimes found between the gaping faucets. That will suffice beneath some roofs —but not ours! Our roof has personality! Quickly recognizing its impotence against the elements, our roof turns with vengeful viciousness upon us, harboring bitterness, I suppose, for having been awkwardly shapened and nailed in place, and exposed to the wind and the rain. Of course, we are helpless. There is just no escaping our sentence. We through raincoats and towels, field jackets, trousers, and canvas bags, over the mosquito netting, hide beneath the blankets and curse the fates.

Well, Bethy, despite these first two and a half pages, I'm still sane and missing you. Your letters have stopped coming, but your last few weeks at Michigan must have been hectic and crowded, at once happy and sad, for familiar places, old friends, and pleasant memories, are hard to leave behind.

Now I have to take it all back and apologize for my haste. You see, Bethy, several days have elapsed since I finished that last paragraph, for the lights went out on the night I began this letter, and right in the middle of that downpour! In the interim, I received a long, newsy letter from you, written somewhere between Ann Arbor and Chicago.

As much as I liked that letter, Bethy—and I thought it was a wonderful letter—you covered everything I recall mentioning in my own letter, the one to which you refer, so thoroughly, that I cannot possibly commit myself without being wide open to the most embarrassing accusations. Before getting tangled up in explanations, perhaps I had better take my own advice and change the subject.

Because our work has taken up all our spare time recently, there are no new outings worthy of mention. I've fallen heir to an additional assignment in the past week that calls for a lot more work, but hold real promise. It puts me in the center of things in a way that I hadn't anticipated in my wildest speculation.

Bethy, the rather awkward advice I volunteered concerning your interest in coming overseas was offered in all possible good faith. However, if you can arrange to come to China---under those circumstances—it's all automatically rescinded. Otherwise, and I betray the most blatant selfishness, I think the advice is well founded!

Enclosed is documentary evidence of the unbounded good will of my esteemed associates. With such recommendations as this one, there's just no predicting the heights the future holds.

My love,

Frosty

"War Department Prepares to Set Example for U.S. in Rehiring of Discharged Veterans."

N.Y. Times 7/24/1945.

Kunming, China
24 July 1945

Dearest Bethy,

This is an incredibly antiquated typewriter. I warn you at the outset of its unpredictable antics in order to testify to my own soberness. In fact, anything appearing in this letter that you take objection to just blame on the machine, for if the intentions of the typist and the written product of this machine agree, it's the purest of coincidence.

In ways this typewriter typifies China. I have great sympathy for the Chinese. But it is nonetheless true that they sustain a 17th century civilization, all of which means that people, nation, and typewriter are about equally modern.

Your letters come regularly, Bethy, and they are always welcome and warming in every way. They are, more importantly, excellent. That's why I value them so highly. In the last one to arrive, you enclosed three snapshots---two of dubious merit, but one superb shot of a very handsome Great Dane. The technique of the latter shot is rather poor, considering the fact that only half the beast is showing, but the background is both interesting and well chosen. The buildings appear to be part of the Michigan campus, and the dog is nicely set off by an extremely attractive fur coat. I would venture that the photographer shows some promise, despite the badly centered subject.

I can't be serious this evening, Bethy. I have just finished a bridge game, one of those strange garbles where the least worthy player, after an evening of inexcusable errors, walks off with all the money, having played with the right partner at the right time. But I've strayed from the subject. I really thought the pictures were swell, and included two of them in my wallet for handy reference.

You can see by now, Bethy, that I'm waging a losing fight with this blasted typewriter. Retribution I suppose for not having looked up my pen.

When you get to San Francisco, you'll be back in my favorite city. It's a shame that the Conference couldn't have lasted a little longer, for you might have had the opportunity of meeting Gene… He would have been delighted to have had the chance to know you. After having come no closer than a telephone conversation in Washington, and after having heard me speak of you so often. He probably would have recognized you in the midst of the busy whirl on Market Street itself.

Legally---and I expect no puns---I am an adult tomorrow. It looks as if I'll always be a junior to you, McGee, not only because of that year's difference in age, but also because you're aging much faster than I.

This really shouldn't be a new paragraph since the subject remains unchanged. It's just this confounded typewriter! The paper fell out just as I reached the punch line which, of course, has now lost its punch. The 21st birthday business is actually an empty technicality. True, it brings with it the opportunity to vote, so that from now on one vote in the Church family will simply cancel out another [Frank Church's father was a Republican]. Outside of that, and that alone, tomorrow will simply serve to emphasize the fact that by the time I have a college diploma, you'll have a tottering old man on your hands. What presumption! What I mean to say is that, at least, I'll be a tottering old man.

Will you have a chance to see Helen…? She's my old flame, you know. If you do, give her the best of good wishes from her old debating partner.

Bethy, of all the beauty spots in the United States, the coastal region about Carmel by the Sea is the most appealing I know of. Carmel, as I remember it, looks out upon the Pacific from the wooded hills of the West Coast. A devourer of the ocean breeze, and situated amidst a plenitude of greenery, I recall Carmel as a veritable Shangri-La. You would like it there, Bethy, if you have the chance to make a side-trip over a weekend.

Since we have been tied down with work for several weeks, there's nothing in the way of news to relate. However, and I think now of Mother's undying curiosity, you may be interested in hearing something of my friends here. Tad..., whose name betrays his Serbian extraction, has become my closest friend of the group. Our work is the same, our schedule is the same, and our disposition sufficiently at variance to make for compatibility. Tad had a football scholarship to the University of Washington, where he credited himself with an enviable record. As a boy of eight years youth, he suffered the misfortune of being left completely bald by a serious case of diphtheria. This has given him the appearance of a Russian Field Marshall which provides him with the advantage of a rather imposing presence. He held the Pacific Northwest heavyweight boxing title, having some 54 Kos and no losses in 58 amateur matches, and having even managed to win a decision from the national Golden Gloves champion in an exhibition bout shortly after entering the Service. So you can see that we are about as much alike as night and day.

Another of my roommates, Earl...lived in Ann Arbor and was in attendance at the University of Michigan, studying in the graduate school for a doctorate in English literature. He is quite talented in diversified ways. During the depression, Earl painted signs for a living. He is equally competent at lettering, at cartoons, or at formal portraits. More importantly, Earl shows real promise in the field of creative writing. Having also an avid interest in politics, we manage to hit it off quite well.

The hour is late, Bethy, and I have a lecture to prepare for the morrow. Until next time, make the best of San Francisco.

Ally my love,

Frosty

"Four million troops, about 2,500,000 from Europe and 1,500,000 from the Pacific and the Far East, will be returned to the United States by June 30..."

N.Y. Times 8/21/1945

**Kunming, China
21 August 1945**

Dearest Bethy,

Upon my return to Kunming, my sojourn into China being happily interrupted by the ending of the war, I found a long twenty-four page letter from you awaiting me. It now is at the right of the same antiquated typewriter I wrote my last letter to you with. I'll refer to it, and should time permit, subject you to the burden of a long-winded analysis, if such it can be called, on issues of domestic and international concern. What a vain beginning this is! Perhaps I had better temper it by turning first to more personal topics.

Your vacation in San Francisco sounds wonderful. I only wish we might be there together. As mentioned in another letter, San Francisco is my favorite city, and there would be many a haunt or better an establishment, where we could have a whale of a good time. Your visits to the art exhibits, to the sculpture displays, to the musicals, although undoubtedly in the company of one of credible merit, nonetheless provokes considerable jealousy from this corner. I should like to have substituted in Phil's place. Besides, if I have anything to contribute in the way of politics, you certainly could instruct me in the field of artistic appreciation. What in hell is Beethoven's "Quartet in A Major Opus 18, No 5"?? Sounds like a code index system, doesn't it?

Your boyfriend---get that, Bethy, the promiscuity is getting out of hand---your admiring "steady," what else can I say, returned to Kunming to find he had passed the acid test, and had received his promotion to First Lieutenant. I was lucky enough to get under the rope just before the war ended, thus avoiding the subsequent freezing of all promotions. Censorship still prevents mention of what I have been doing, or what the immediate plans for the future are. However, as regards the latter, even if regulations were relaxed, things are in such a state of flux that I wouldn't hazard a prediction. Tragically enough, it is certain that my feeble number of points hold no promise of an early release from the service. And that's that, however much I regret it.

Aunt Eve ever hopeful of returning me to the straight and narrow, sent me an envelope of clippings from home periodically during the past months. I suppose the practice will continue since here selection of articles provides sufficient antagonism to arouse me from an ever-growing lethargy, to furnish a spark of renewed interest that gives me cause to ask for more. She faithfully sends me Congressman Dworshak's [later Frank Church's Senate colleague] Capital Greetings, a weekly publication that reflects both the dullness and vacuousness that characterize his tenure in Congress. And she also sends me those little gems [Idaho author] Vardis Fisher sells to the Idaho Sunday Statesman. There are infuriating. It would be interesting to run a feature debate with Fisher in an opposite column in the Statesman, although that paper would certainly never sanction such a proposal. But let me stray from the subject.

I've been seeing a good number of pictures lately. They are wearisome largely because they totally lack any evidence of originality. You are familiar with the common Hollywood patterns. What is most provoking, to my way of thinking, is the invariable "Fairytale Ending." Now this is a sore point, I realize. But, Bethy, something must be critically wrong with the popular American tastes that make it necessary to contort and sugar-coat every legitimate story to appease the public. It's sickening! We are rapidly degenerating into a nation of soft-hearted, weak-minded, sentimentalists. Why must every scoundrel, in a character role, be brought to justice? That's not true to life. Why must every romance be legitimate? Why must every policeman win the most attractive maiden with an invisible halo? I might put it in stronger language, but to be decent, it's possible to carry standards of propriety to the point of sterility, and that's just what's happening to the movies. If the cinema must be a vehicle for soothing escape, let it at least be a virile escape!

Well back to the subject of political economy. Remember, Bethy, this is not an imposition of my own choosing. Your request, made on repeated occasions, must answer for whatever patient perseverance necessary to wade through the following tirade:

I am fearful that the United States is about to launch itself into a program of unprecedented imperialism. The indications are everywhere apparent, the reasons somewhat more difficult to discern. I think there are two basic causes, one purely economic, the other political. The former being the more important, for the political is largely its logical reflection, let's consider the first.

To begin with, in order to clear the decks for avoiding confusing terminology, especially those high-sounding phrases that carry moral connotation, it's important to call a stone a stone. Our economic system is not free enterprise. It has been increasingly less so since the turn of the century. Our system is a highly industrialized, complex system of capitalism, limited only by certain inadequate public control. Such a system, dependent as it is upon the accumulation of profit, functions successfully---but not necessarily justly---in an expanding economy. The term "an expanding economy" has been subjected to more abuse and misinterpretation than any I know. It should be clarified. If I am producing print dresses for a profit, I must produce a sufficient number to be sold at a sufficiently high price so that the costs of labor and material can be met without selling the whole number. It is the sale of the excess number that makes for the profit. In other words, the amount of money I pay out will not buy back all that is manufactured. And a market must be found for the surplus. The larger the profit, the larger the margin of difference between production and purchasing power. When the market can be found, profit is realized, and the reinvested into plant expansion and new industry, thus increasing production once again. The problem re-occurs: New markets must be found to absorb the margin of surplus.

This necessity for an expanding market is not at all peculiar to the United States. In fact, we encountered it much later than the

European nations largely because we were a young, and vigorous, and growing nation. The population was rapidly increasing, the open frontier was being pushed steadily west. When maladjustments occurred, those were left jobless, or those who refused to accept the "sweat shop," could move out to the free land, could settle on homesteads of their own, could seek out new mines of silver, copper, and gold, new employment, and test their luck in the booming, lawless West. The expanding market was a domestic one, and capitalism, with all its unbridled ruthlessness, did more to develop America than any other possible device. Individualism, in its loosest form---for it was genuine free enterprise---brought to America a Golden Age.

But an end had to come as it had come much earlier in Europe. We soon had to find a foreign market, and we sought to secure that market, in some cases, by fighting Spain, thus securing possession of the Philippines, and political control over the West Indies. We penetrated South America economically and then politically. Our flurry of imperialism was modest as compared to that of England and France, but then our need was not so urgent.

Today, we face the most critical need of our history. To maintain the present level of employment, it follows that we must also maintain our present level of production. The demand that created that level of production was the Second World War. The market that will maintain it is being sought in foreign investment and foreign sales. This is the easiest way out. It is also the way of futility and eventual conflict. I don't for a minute oppose international trade done on a reciprocal basis. Such agreements can be mutually profitable, and they can be partly stabilized and controlled. But business fully understands that it must have, in order to avoid ruin, or the acceptance of further government bonds, a favorable balance of trade, which means control of foreign markets, and a high, protective tariff. If we accept this course, as we appear to be doing, where will it lead us?

If we allow it to, such a course directly leads to political penetration backed up with actual or threatened military protection. Imperialism, in its blackest and most dangerous form! What follows happened in Mexico a few years ago. Anxious for the welfare of its own people, and in quest of economic independence, the Mexican Government confiscated, or better appropriated both the American and British oil fields. England broke off diplomatic relations, causing a serious crisis, while the United States, believing the Good Neighbor policy more important, decided to register only an official protest. Where the stakes are higher, a similar incident elsewhere will lead to very real trouble.

Besides, such a course is only a temporary stop-gap, even if we dominate for a time. Even if, as in the case of China, let's suppose the penetration takes a much milder form. Let's suppose that the Chinese government arranges for its own people to accept large American investments in the form of loans, the Chinese retaining the control of their industries, upon the promise of 6% interest. In a little time, the profits achieved will be used by the Chinese to buy out the American interest entirely, so that we will have to seek investment elsewhere, and see it in an ever diminishing sphere. The problem isn't solved, but complicated.

There is only one other alternative. The high purchasing level must be found at home! How? I think there are three methods, all of which combined will not be entirely satisfactory, but will certainly constitute a great help.

1. A variable tax program that will more heavily tax profits in periods of relative prosperity, and relax the rate during periods of regression. Thus, the amount of money to be reinvested could be held within reasonable limits, while the additional federal funds could be held as a reserve for temporary relief.

2. The extension of the power of the Federal Government to include, if necessary, the licensing of industry in order to stamp out monopoly wherever it exists. Competition must be revived for it will help to keep prices down, and to promote increased efficiency.

3. The public support and protection of independent labor unions, with the strongest encouragement for a wholesale house-cleaning of the unions themselves. The union monopolies ought to be broke up too, although I fear that any such attempt would split the Liberal camp wide open, subjecting it to drastic political defeat. Healthy, responsible unions will help to maintain high wages, or putting it another way, high purchasing power. In this connection, the government should extend all practicable assistance to small businesses, where the remnants of free enterprise survive, and to co-operatives, where profits are distributed among the members, and where an approach to economic democracy is to be found.

This is a treatise of dubious merit, and it must come to an end before I put you to sleep. As I look over the above three proposals, I am surprised to find how conservative they really are. However, such a platform can be realized if the Liberals can ever get together. It's compromise program, and that, I believe is to its credit, for the extreme reaction in either the direction of the Right or Left will mean authoritarian government, the kind we must, if possible, prevent.

Bethy, I hope this war, now that it has ended, will not prevent my return to civilian status for too long a time. I'm aching to see you again soon. So chin up---

With love,

Frosty

"Pearl Harbor Data Called 'Whitewash."

N.Y. Times 9/6/1945

"The Atomic Age began at exactly 5:30 mountain war time on the morning of July 16, 1945, on a stretch of semi-desert land about 50 airline miles from Alamogordo, N.M., just a few minutes before the dawn of a new day on this earth."

N.Y. Times 9/6/1945

China
6 September 1945

Dearest Bethine,

The passing days have slowly brought home to me something of the full impact those foreboding events of the month past project upon us all. Slowly I have come to realize that there is no longer an exit from fact, no longer room for convenient self-delusion. We must, and Bethy, I cannot submit this too earnestly, discard as quickly as the inertia of a people permits the whole compound of inhibition, distrust, and timidity, characterizing our national attitude, and that of the entire world.

I really don't mean to lecture. I don't want to sound pompous. The truth is that writing you provides me, among other compensations, with an outlet for putting down, however awkwardly, those few intense, deep-rooted beliefs that pry open containment, and command expression. Better that I fumble out than attempt to shackle them, for to do so would require more willpower than I can readily muster.

There are few endeavors more worthy than that of preventing war. I felt, until a month ago---yet hardly believed, that the common need for peace might avert the sudden outbreak of new war for many years ahead. I knew there could be no lasting peace because nations, jealously guarding their sovereignty, each in pursuit of its own ends, were subservient to no higher authority than their own. There could be no lasting peace because our system of living made war profitable for the few most influential, made war at times essential either to the attainment or to the preservation of wealth and dominance. Finally, primarily, I knew there could be no lasting peace because all peoples were steeped in ideology, the façade for greed, ignorance, prejudice, for distrust, and bigotry, and violent hate. We offered ourselves as bewildered victims in each succeeding massacre.

But the question of war and peace, I now believe, is locked away in the era that marked our youth. The issue is now a very different one, a challenge as simple as it is inescapable, the kind that all must understand. We have left just two choices, life or death. For the love of God let's have the common sense to accept the undeniable!

With few exceptions indeed, people I meet over here speak elatedly of the atomic bomb. There are those who tell me, with an expression of the most revealing astonishment, and with incredulous enthusiasm, that our discovery is as yet so imperfect that only one tenth of one percent of its total explosive energy has thus far been realized. Apparently it is not enough to have at last developed the instrument of our self-destruction. We even applaud approaching doom! And in a way, Bethy, it is fitting retribution. What could be a more proper finale? For centuries we have synthesized the elements to advance the cause of death. Now we can disintegrate the elements and thus approach the infinite. Let us get on with our work. For it is not surprising that mortal civilization should ultimately confirm the triumph of man's intellect, the annihilation of man's soul. [end of letter]

> *"The mighty events which in four crowded months brought about the surrender of both Germany and Japan and put an end to the greatest war that ever-scourged mankind have already made this year of 1945 memorable. But the speed and drama of these events have also tended to obscure the fundamental changes which the war has wrought."*
>
> N.Y. Times 9/9/1945

On 9 September 1945, pursuant to the General Order, Japanese commanders in China and representatives of Generalissimo Chiang signed the Act of Surrender—China Theater in Nanking.

Nanking, China
9 September 1945

Dearest Bethine,

This will be a short letter for it deals with my experience today in Nanking, or better, with those occurring between eight and ten o'clock this morning. You will read in the papers of the General [Yasuji] Okamura's surrender of all Japanese forces in China to Ho Yin-chin, Supreme Commander of the Chinese Armies at 9 o'clock on the ninth day of the ninth month of 1945. Or at least that is probably the way most objective historians will record it. I was lucky enough to be present at the ceremony.

The impressions that I shall probably always retain, other than those of the proceeding itself, will be the festive celebrations, the long columns of Chinese troops, the scattered groups of Japanese soldiers idling confidently, defiantly in the streets. It is strange to find oneself after all these years of war in the midst of the Japanese army, to see Japanese officers riding haughtily on horseback with their attendant guards behind them, to see exited groups of bewildered Chinese, people who seemingly still fear the Japanese, jabbering in the streets, apparently not yet aware of what is really happening.

The surrender took place in a colorfully decorated auditorium at the former Chinese National Military Academy. A long avenue of flags marked the route from the medieval gateway across the park to the auditorium on the opposite end of the court. Surprisingly enough, I had been one of those invited to attend the ceremony, and had a grandstand seat in the balcony directly above the tables upon which the terms of surrender occurred.

The ceremony was as impressive as it was colorful. Red, white, and blue bunting had been carefully hung about the floor, the flags of the United Nations surmounted the platform on either side of a large portrait of Sun Yat Sen, founder of the republic. The Japanese delegation arrived in an attitude of stiff formality. They sat rigidly at the table opposite the Chinese. Upon the receipt of the official papers, General Okamura was required to bow twice, and it appeared to me as if those bows would break his back. He bowed once more upon affixing his signature. During the whole of the proceedings, the Japanese did not speak. A staff officer presented a prepared statement at the outset, and when the papers were signed the enemy delegation was speedily dismissed. They left with expressions of twisted, sour dejection.

It certainly was gratifying to see how difficult, how painfully awkward, the whole ceremony was for the Japanese. And well it might have been. For nine years now, the Japanese have been pushing the Chinese all over the map of China. Not once have their forces suffered a serious defeat. They held all the important regions of China, and their armies were still intact. To have to surrender to the Chinese must have been bitter, indeed.

But it was, nonetheless, a great day for China. And it was amazingly good fortune for me to have been able to witness the event. Someday, if I make no mark anywhere, some Chinese historian will run across my signature on the memorial roster, buried among those of the other guests who were invited to attend. I felt like a member of the chorus, high upon the platform backstage, in one of the finale acts of history.

With love,

Frosty

"There will be a 'hard' peace for Japan...the Allied Reparations Commission."

N.Y. Times 9/22/1945

Nanking, China
22 September 1945

Dear Bethy,

If you will excuse it, Bethy, this letter is going to be about the same as the one I have written to the folks. Censorship has restricted my writing for so long that when the bubble popped I wanted to sit down and write of many things at once. There were, and are, however, too many things to include in one letter. Eight months can't be crowded onto two or three pages. The last few days have played me out so that the course of least resistance is that of describing here the recent events included in my letter home, and to do so---largely because of mental and physical exhaustion—in about the same words. It won't happen again, and I hope you will not mind it just this once.

If there is one axiom applicable to my lifetime with a fixed and consistent persistency, the axiom has been that of extremity. Things have always happened to me in a big way. The good and the bad have come in such generous doses that I'm usually left bewildered in their wake. My "ups" have spiraled into the nebulae, my "downs" to the moldering pits of Hell. It has so far been my good fortune that the "ups" should so greatly out-number the "downs," although if the laws of averages ever begin to take effect, I'm in store for a wretched future.

The above, for what it's worth, is in way of introduction to the long and complicated story of my service in China. The story, as you know, begins in Kunming, the capital city of Yunnan Province, in the "Valley of Eternal Spring." But it's foolish to begin this saga with any reference to the weather, that being the one subject I sued to be able to discuss with impunity in my letters. Better to begin by saying that Kunming lies high in the primitive area of Southwest China. Until the war opened the Burma Road, Kunming had no contact with the outer world, her people being isolated in their mountainous valley. It was an ancient city sprung to life by the influx of Americans and the stimulus of war.

In the first week of May, following our memorable trip across the Road, we were assigned to the G-2 Section, Hqs., Chinese Combat Command. Our work was to be that for which we had been trained, and we were pleased to find it fully as comprehensive and essential as we had been led to anticipate at Ritchie. ... also had an O/B Team, having worked with the command for several months prior to our arrival. With the additional personnel, it was possible to set to work forming an adequate picture of the enemy situation.

For the first two months, I was primarily concerned with the research phase of the work. The reports of my section, in the form of special studies, were sent out periodically to the field commands, to both higher and lower echelon. It kept me busy, for it also involved the processing of many different daily reports for the purpose of building permanent records and files of intelligence value. This doesn't sound romantic or adventuresome, and it wasn't. But the work was absorbing, since the responsibility for tracing the movements of enemy units, together with making new identifications and estimating enemy strength, was ours. The recompense was that of knowing that the work was important, and that those in charge felt it was being handled well.

Then one day in early July, Colonel Hayman, who was at that time the G-2 called me into his office and asked me to prepare the next morning's orientation. These presentations were given each morning in the War Room for the Commanding General and his staff. Major Tussman, my immediate senior, had been giving the G-2 estimate of the situation at these morning conferences, and it was of those "breaks" in the game he should be temporarily called away. A substitute was needed. It just happened that Colonel Hayman decided to try me out.

The orientation went off very well. As a matter of fact, everybody was quite surprised. General McClure and the staff were apparently pleased, for it was privately suggested that I continue to officiate. That's how it all began.

The ramifications were many. After a while, I grew into the job of being the designated spokesman for the G-2 Section. This meant a lot more work---and, Bethy, fewer letters---but I liked it, and could manage it satisfactorily.

Shortly after the end of the war, forward echelon of the headquarters moved to Chihkiang, where preliminary arrangements were made with the Japanese for the final surrender at Nanking. I was sent along to be the acting G-2. Things were informal and very pleasant. Every morning, I would go over to the General's quarters with my portable situation map, and present the most recent developments. The General, usually in his undershirt, would draw up a chair for a private session that would last from ten to twenty minutes. We became quite well acquainted.

I arrived in Nanking in time for the surrender. My last letter had to do with the details of the conference, the festivities of the day, and the peculiar circumstances that made the surrender one of the most dramatic in history. We were kept busy, following the ceremony, setting up offices and getting settled once again. Nanking brought with it our first contact with Western civilization. We are billeted here in the Metropolitan Hotel. Our officer club is housed in an elaborate building formerly used by the Chinese government for state occasions, while several night clubs in the city are now open for our use. We are seeing China's cleaner face.

But to get back to the narrative, three nights ago I was surprised to receive a telephone call from General McClure's quarters. He invited me to dinner, and although I would like to deal at length with the evening's events, time and space don't permit it, and I'll have to leave the affair largely to your imagination. There were six Colonels present, six Colonels and a First Lieutenant. The General's residence is the late Manchukuo Embassy, a lavish place very richly furnished. For some astonishing reason, and, Bethy, I own that this is a strange story, the General chose to treat me as the guest of honor, much to the understandable dismay of the others. He introduced me as the man with the finest diction in the Army, and during the course of the evening asked me to read aloud one of his favorite stories. I mention this in particular not because it made me feel like the court jester, as it did, but rather because it led to an invitation to accompany the General on a special trip to Hangchow, a trip that was to prove the most fabulous of my experience. An account of this trip, completed yesterday, is really the purpose of this letter, in spite of the fact that I've taken a long time to get to it.

First of all, there were only three in the American party—the General, his aide-de-camp, Captain Ownes, and I. We joined General Ho Yin-chin, Supreme Commander of the Chinese Army, and his staff at the airport. We flew to Hanchow in Chiang Kai Shek's personal plane, and there the festivities began.

It was General Ho's triumphant entry into the city. A regiment of troops greeted us at the field as the guard of honor, and the formal inspection over, we were carried into the city in an entourage of gaily decorated automobiles. The streets were jammed with shouting people. Flags hung low over the crowded street. Exploding firecrackers and aerial bombs sounded loudly everywhere. And General McClure stole the show. Stopping at irregular intervals, he would stoop to pat some half-frightened, half-bewildered child lightly on the cheek until finally a bold Galahad, a cute little youngster in a scout uniform, strode forward into the middle of the street to shake the General's hand. In the midst of each episodes as these, we would fall behind the official party and soon be lost in the crowd. Everything would stop when the frantic guards were sent back to find McClure. Thus, for nearly an hour, we paraded through the streets of Hangchow.

Our destination was the residence of the Provincial Governor, where a reception was held in the garden during the afternoon for the press and the city's distinguished citizens. We were to stay at the Governor's palace for the whole of our visit.

That evening we attended a dinner of honor given in an auditorium in the middle of the city. It was an Oriental feast I'll long remember. If numbers matter, there were between nineteen and twenty-four courses, fresh shrimp, cracked crab, roasted duck served in its own broth, spiced chicken, sweet and sour pork, sword fish stomach, and countless other delicacies I couldn't possibly name, let alone remember.

It is a venerable old Chinese custom to drink toasts to one another throughout a meal. Soon you are caught up in the spirit of the thing so that it seems inconceivable that hot wine should be drunk in any other way. The first toasts are formal, conventional. The Generalissimo and President Truman took first precedent, and then in order, the most distinguished guests. But soon the toasts became spontaneous. As the wine goes down, formality disappears, and everybody begins to enjoy himself. Soon General Ho was on his feet proposing a toast to me, and I one to him, the only difference being that the junior member of such an exchange must "gambei," or drink his whole cupful, while the senior member may sip as he chooses. I came out on the long end of the exchange.

The banquet over, we returned to the Governor's palace for dancing. Left were only twelve of us in the party, and we found upon our arrival twelve very lovely girls from the city's best families. The dance lasted until midnight, being interrupted for hot coffee and French pastries at hourly respites.

But the evening was far from over. Hangchow is both the Niagara Falls and Venice of China. Her West Lake, filled with gondolas, is the honeymoon paradise for the fortunate newlyweds who can visit the city. And we had arrived on the celebrated night of the harvest moon. Naturally, therefore, the evening had to include a trip on the lake. We were rowed out to an island of lotus blossoms, resplendent in the phosphorescent glow of the harvest moon. I told the Mayor that I should like to spend my honeymoon in Hangchow on the lake, and he assured me that if I would telegraph ahead, he would come to Shanghai to welcome me.

[*As Chairman of the U.S. Senate Foreign Relations Committee, Frank Church led the first Senate delegation to visit Shanghai and Beijing after the U.S. recognized the People's Republic of China in 1979.*]

The Mayor, incidentally, is a graduate of MIT, having received his degree in Boston in 1919. He was the Generalissimo's private secretary during the war, speaks flawless English, and appointed himself as personal host to Captain Ownes and I during our three-day visit. He's a grand fellow, and showed us a wonderful time. On the following evening, after another sumptuous feast on the lakeshore, the Mayor and I, if you can imagine, sang the "Strawberry Blonde" and "I Want a Gal Just Like the Gal Who Married Dear Old Dad" all the way back to the Governor's palace. Bethy, it was like a tale from the Arabian nights.

So many things happened in the next two days that I couldn't include them all here, especially in a letter that has already spread its limits. The trip is over, and we've returned laden with gifts and good tidings.

I have some gifts for you, Bethy, that I believe you will like, at least I hope so. Some, I may send by mail, but several will probably be brought back safe hand with "the body."

With apologies for the bravado------------

All my love,

Frosty

"Winning the Peace: 'It Is Our Job'; We have the first responsibility to fashion a structure to fit the new world environment."

N.Y. Times 9/30/1945

Nanking, China
30 September 1945

Dear Bethy,

This afternoon I shouldn't write this letter. My determined fight against another cold has met with its customary failure. As a consequence, I am confined to my room feeling very sorry for myself, and very badly about the immediate prospects that lie ahead. You, Bethy, of all people, will understand how I feel. I am now, by the grace of God, twenty-one years of age, and, judging from the way I feel this afternoon, it will take considerably more than the grace of God to keep me alive another twenty-one years. It is going on three years now that I've floundered in the Army. The war is over. It took me out of my freshman year in college, and a man has a right to get back to his pursuits. I want to begin to live!

But that doesn't much affect the Army. The Army has a system. Of course, it isn't a simple efficient system. That would never do! It is a grandiose mathematical nightmare, a ludicrous abortion that proves to me once and for all that figures lie. It should be admitted that the Army tried to be fair. In fact the Army tried so hard to be fair, that it forgot to be reasonable. If you know the system, Bethy, then you will agree with me that while the war was still in progress, it was proper to dismiss on a basis of points, the minority of men who were scheduled to be released. But now the war is over, and one would presume that the Army would decide at once how many men should stay, and in China that number would be negligible, and then proceed to assemble the surplus as quickly as they are released from their organization, and ship them out on all available ships and planes. Why, Bethy, three ships the size of the Queen Mary could evacuate in a single voyage all American personnel in China.

It goes without saying that the Army would be the last agency in the world to adopt so logical a course. "Men with high point scores must go first!" (But there aren't enough such men being declared surplus to fill the planes. So, the planes fly the Hump half empty!) "Men with low scores will be used to replace men with high scores!" (Nonsense! Those now qualified by points to leave are being held up awaiting replacements, who, upon arriving have little to do but sit and wait for their replacement. The paper work is naturally all bogged down, so the planes and ships leave half empty). But the system will live---God bless it! ---so long as the Army continues to dominate at home. I don't see how I can be home by Christmas. I doubt if I can make it before Easter.

There is another reason for my dejection. It's been over a month now since I've heard from you. But I think it's due to bad mail service, although that scarcely helps to give voice to silence. I hope this problem corrects itself soon.

Bethy, have you gotten a job? Are you to become a woman of leisure? Are you going to remain in Boise for a time? Have you learned to cook---yet? Are you continuing your sculpture? Have you seen Helen? How about Mother and Dad? How about Eva? Uncle Bern? How about Terry? Do you still love "Fairy Tale" endings? This war should discourage even your faith in that direction, at least as collective cases go. Is your figure as pretty as ever! The snapshots you sent exposed very little more than a fur coat. How is the Judge? How is Mrs. Clark? You may notice, Bethy, that these questions are hardly in what would be considered "proper" order. I just put them down as they occurred to me, and the reason for their sequence has more to do with some things I wanted to say next, and consequently put down in the form of questions first, than anything else.

Something tragic happened, and I'm not to blame. After keeping your "Modesty" pinned on the door of my locker back in Kunming, it was soaked in a leaking trunk on a trip to Kweiyang just before the ending of the war. And your "Modesty" is spoiled, Bethy. I hope you have another picture for me at home.

If Helen ever mentions my exceedingly infrequent letters, will you apologize for me? Every time I write Helen, I'm all wrapped up about something and mange to explode. My letters are sermons to be burned or spurned, as you like it. I'm planning to write Helen a simple, friendly letter soon.

I am enclosing some pictures of myself to illustrate the fact that I haven't gained a pound of weight in nearly three years. There seems to be a growing prospect, or so it's encouraging to believe, of obtaining a medical discharge for being excessively under-weight. As a matter of less selfish interest, you will also find some photographs of my recent trip to Hangchow with the necessary explanations on the backs.

Bethy, I hope you will write me about yourself, what you've been doing since leaving California, who you've seen of our friends—both present and erstwhile---and above all, of what you think about anything or everything. And Bethy, if you disagree with me, say so in as strong language as I have attempted to affirm any questions at issue. Nothing is so stimulating as intellectual disagreement, when arguments on both sides are creditable. If mine are not, tell me so, and why.

Tonight, General Boatner, our deputy commander, is giving a farewell party for himself. It's nearly time for me to make an attempt to attend, so I must close---

With much love,

Frosty

"November Redeployment Upped to 47,000 Men; More Vessels Promised."

N.Y. Times 10/18/1945

```
                                    Nanking, China
                                    18 October 1945
```

[*Dear Bethy*]

When the Army sets out to achieve an objective, it always takes a long time to get things in motion. But once things begin to roll, the job is done on a grand scale, and with much less delay than one accustomed to Army procedures would expect. At first, American soldiers were leaving China at snail's pace, but now between four and six hundred a day are being flown over the "Hump" into India. Preparations for opening a separation center in Shanghai are near completion. The aerial route should close out by the end of this month, the plan being that those of us who still remain in China will then be systematically released through the port at Shanghai. "Nearly all American troops," we are told, will be enroute home from China by Christmas of this year. That's the target date, and it looks as though it may be met.

However, Bethy, I believe I'm to be given the keys with which to lock up the last American installation here in China, and although the general picture is bright, I doubt that I'll be back by Christmas. The next best plan is to send Christmas home to you. There some things I've packed up in Nanking and elsewhere during the last four weeks that I hope you'll like. Shopping for them has been fascinating. The accomplished purchases and the veteran merchants in this country make each exchange a time honored ceremony. The battle of wits begins as soon as you enter a shop. Sensing what you want most to buy, the proprietor will price the article at twice the intended value. As loudly as the merchant praises the article does the purchaser then proceed to condemn it. Both parties are soon caught up in the spirit of the bargaining, and it then becomes a contest of bluff and endurance. Most frequently the merchant, being the more experienced, wins out, but occasionally he becomes so anxious to make the sale---feeling, I suppose, that thirty minutes effort is completely lost should he fail to make the sale. ---that he ends up by awarding the article in question at a third of its original price. Shopping thus has become a challenge to both parties adding materially to the color and interest of the hunt.

One of the advantages of our new station in Nanking is the excellent food. We are no longer dependent upon the limited produce of the crowded interior, supplemented by dehydrated rations flown in from India. Food is plentiful here. The Army has set up its own slaughterhouse making meat abundant. The excellence of the food, happily enough, applies to the restaurants in town as well, so that we can mix Chinese with American meals at pleasure, and feel equally well satisfied. This is a lot of space devoted to the subject of food, Bethy. It's just that after so long in China, a person gets stomach conscious.

Your descriptions of the [Robinson] "Bar" were marvelous. Caramba! It would be swell to spend some time back in the hills of Idaho. Bethy, I believe that those of us who have not only grown up in Idaho, but who have also had the chance to know the State, never lose the attachment we hold for it. Wherever else we may live, however fond we may become of another place, or many others, there lingers an appetite only Idaho can appease, and your letter touched that spot. Stevenson expressed it well for it's a fact the inherent and spontaneous sentiment, "Home is the sailor, home from the sea, and the hunter, home from the hill."

Well, before I break down and cry, let's turn to the subject of Nanking, China, without so much as the passing thought that it lies on the opposite side of the globe. Nanking is an ancient city, a fact that certainly fails to distinguish it from any other city in China. But at least it is one of many to retain many symptoms of its age. The city has not yet outgrown the area inscribed by the great wall surrounding it. Any approach into the city must be made through one of several gates. These gates are easily forty feet thick, and present a formidable appearance from every angle. Mounted in concrete above each is a circular sheet of brass, the signal gong for sounding the alarm of an imminent attack upon the city.

Of course, parts of Nanking are fully Westernized. The public buildings, completed by the Chinese government shortly before Japanese troops occupied the city, are modernistic in design. These buildings reflect no suggestion of the distinctive and traditional style, long separating the building of China from those of any other civilization. I hate to see the gradual deterioration of national cultures. In our grandchildren's day, I'm afraid there will be little less variety in a trip from Indianapolis to Chicago, than in one from Agra to Timbuctoo. And mountains look about the same anywhere.

Bethy, if my luck is good I might be out of the Army next April or May. How about a date for a shopping trip? I'll need advice about civilian suits. Who can tell? Without your guidance, I might even buy a brown one!

Love,

Frosty

"In signing the protocol U.S. Secretary of State Byrnes said the Charter was now a 'part of the law of nations' and that it was a 'memorable day for the peace-loving peoples of all nations.'

N.Y. Times 10/24/1945

On Oct. 24, 1945, the United Nations charter took effect.

Oct. 24, 1945

Dear Frosty,

Yes, my dearest, I still believe in "Fairy Tales." My specialty is happy endings. You sounded very low, but don't be! Any minute now you'll be back and getting started and all of China will be a wonderful memory of places, events, happenings. The struggle and the lonesomeness will be the part of the very dim past.

Of course, you should write me when you're blue. I'm the crazy dope who still is sure there must be a rhyme and reason in it all. Sometimes I'm so afraid of the open way I phrase and feel things that I just don't let loose. Besides, your cold and blue feeling will no doubt be over by the time you receive this, and it will seem rather silly. That's the trouble. If I could reach across all of that space just at the moment I'm needed it would be super, but by the time the mail answers, the moment has passed.

Anyway, Frosty, when you laugh at my ideas of life you laugh at all that helps what you once called my "inevitable smile," remember? Well, you see here I sit in indecision—nothing in my life is very sure except tomorrow, and an extreme pessimist doubts even that, but anyway there's no use sitting still and feeling blue, though I do when things like colds, teeth, etc. are there to add to my being down. I've been just bugging around enjoying people and things and praying I shall never be a sourpuss. Perhaps that's why you mean what you do to me. You smile and enjoy life, and in the midst of any pessimistic feeling you still seem to like people.

I'm sure that I don't know what life will bring, but it's been rather wonderful—I've had my ears knocked down but people like our folks—my roommates Helen, Gusty, etc;--ad infinitum (I know nothing of Latin) even they make me believe in the underlying goodness in things.

Sometimes I feel foolish about you—you sign your letters love and talk about reunion in Mexico, etc. yet you've said nothing of loving me. Life is silly. I've never written such things because letters are easily misunderstood and vulnerable, but I'll take a chance. You sounded so sort of lost. You want me to tell you about myself...well this is part of my doubts and wonders. But, actually it ceased to worry me. If time comes when a thing should be, it probably---if not, not---and that makes me very nearly a fatalist. That may be what I'm coming to, but at any rate I've never seen anyone sit down doing nothing, or on the other hand, push and force something that got anywhere any quicker. Living life just as it comes and getting the most of it by giving as much as possible to it is all I can believe.

In some ways this has been an unproductive summer—no job—little "cooking"—and yet I've done many new things and known many new people. I have started a new statue and I'm hoping to get a model I can use without scandalizing any of the town folk.

I just got back to Boise this afternoon from Salt Lake. I spent a week with Beulah, bought new glasses and a flame colored, very plain wool dress. As to my figure---you'll have to come see for yourself---[illegible]

Love, Bethy

"Marshall Outlines Security Needs..."

"The United States Government and industrial corporations should move slowly in extending *loans to China...former U.S. Ambassador.*"

N.Y. times 11/14/1945

November 14, 1945

Dear Frosty,

I'm tired of writing to you. When I have something to say, I want to tell you. For example, I'm so excited about my packages from China, only I'll wait for Christmas, but then I don't want to thank you on paper. I want to thank you!

Frosty, guess what happened tonight? I got lost—yes in Boise. You see I was to go to an Association of University Women's meeting and was a little early so I decided to walk (the folks [Judge and Mrs. Clark] are in court in Moscow). I went over to find the 300 block of Franklin. It isn't there—it turns into Fort. Well I should have come home, but it was a lovely, crisp, starry night and I crossed the canal looking for it. I found a shaggy dog and his name became "Butch," and we walked down gravel roads, missed puddles by inches, and I protected him from dogs. What a comfort he was---scared of his own shadow. Finally, after an hour I found an end of Franklin, but it was too late so I started home. Just then I found that Butch had a collar, and we walked back to the house where I'd met him. I knocked and asked the lady if he was hers? Sure enough, and she had to hold him to keep him from following. She said it was funny because he didn't usually like strangers. His name was "Brownie" instead of "Butch"---at heart I figure he must of felt himself "Butch." Anyway, I hadn't felt like going to the meeting, so I slipped into comfortable clothes, turned on the radio, and settled down.

[*Bob Wardwell was one of the group of high school friends including Carl Burke, Stan Burns, Wade Fleetwood who would gather after high school at Governor Clark's house, 109 W. Idaho St. in Boise. Bob Wardwell, whose plane was named "Clarky's Kitchen," was killed when a different plane he was piloting crashed in Japan.*]

I wrote the hardest letters I've ever written—one to Helen… and one to Mrs. Donovan.… I loved him so Frosty, that only in that can I sense … great loss. I can't explain it, but I worried about Bobby most and wrote him very regularly. He has taught me a little of what it means to have a true and wonderful friend. I know just one is worth any other disillusionment and should be cherished. I shall miss him. People think I'm cold because I go on speaking of him just as I did, but Bobby's picture lies with those who loved him. I sent Helen…Aiken's poem, "Bread and Music"---it fits so beautifully.

I felt terrible until Mom and I went over it all. I had a letter written on the 18th, and he crashed on the 19th. He had received a letter from the Bar and said that in his restless movement and flying, he was so busy keeping alive, he'd forgotten what peace was. But that my letter had reminded him of "God's in his heaven, all's right with the world." It was so strangely prophetic a letter somehow. Bobby had no goal, no surety, but he was wonderful, and I can hardly believe it yet.

We just came back from the ranch. Beulah and I took a cousin from New York to look at it. It was wonderful, snow laden---truly the setting for snow bound—six below one morning, fifteen below one other. A boy just liberated from Wake Island prisoners who were held in Shanghai and Japan for four years went with us. He used to be a mining engineer up above the dredge above the ranch, and went with a cousin of mine. He was just like a kid at getting back and luckily, he got his buck—a beautiful big four pointer and was thrilled.

We went in swimming—the hot water surrounded by snow. About seven or eight people from around heard Beulah was there and dropped in for dinner. We ended up with quite a party. It certainly was even more cut off from the world than usual. It certainly was a wonderful trip.

I'll write again soon in a less jumbled fashion, but for now remember that to you,

My love,

Bethy

"Army Returning 500,000 From Europe This Month; Expects to Catch Up With All 'Availables' by Jan.15."

N.Y. Times 11/18/1945

Shanghai, China
18 November 1945

My Dearest Bethine,

I've been looking for someone to kick me hard in the pants. There's no excuse in the world for my having written you in so despondent a time, or for having troubled you with whimpers and complaints. You have put up with enough without having to shoulder the additional burden of my very bad disposition. I apologize, Bethy, and promise to write only when I have the "smiles" and the "blues."

Despite all the teasing, Bethy, I think your ideas on life perfectly wonderful. I don't laugh at them—I envy them. Mind you, young lady, they are not entirely realistic---you insist on giving to many people the benefit of every doubt---but that simply adds to their luster. The "inevitable smile" is one of many reasons I'm so very fond of you, one of many reasons you mean so very much to me. You must know, Bethy, that I want, that I have wanted all these months, to put it more strongly than that. How often I've longed to draw you very close to me, to tell you I was deeply and passionately in love with you. Nothing would make me happier that to do just that, and yet, at other times, the thought of it makes me so uneasy, sometimes almost embarrassed.

Then I'm uncertain and provoked---not at you, at myself---and I feel that I have no right to encourage you. But I can never bring myself to discourage you. You are the only girl I've really ever cared for. You are the only girl I have ever wanted to love.

I hope you won't say "That's all fine, but you therefore don't love me." Bethy, if I knew that it wasn't there, if I were even partly sure that I'm not or will not soon be in love with you in a way open to no uncertainty, I would tell you so now. I'll never be dishonest about it, in fairness to you, I just have to become certain of it.

That's the reason, I suppose, that my letters have been filled with everything but you, and my feelings toward you. And, it's the reason I've signed—or failed to sign—"love" and the reason I've jabbered about reunions in Mexico, half-trying to let you know that I've no right to say that I do love you.

Does this make any sense? Probably it does. When it comes to you, I always bungle things, and this letter is probably a masterpiece of bungling. At least, it may help to answer a few questions without provoking many more. Perhaps it helps explain why I am so anxious to get home.

There really isn't much else I want to write about right now, Bethy. A lot has happened recently. The big chapter of my overseas service is closed. I'm in Shanghai with a new assignment, a wholly different kind of job, serving as a stop-gap until my turn rolls around for returning home. Having just 51 points, it's not likely that I'll get away before the first of the year.

Enclosed is the citation accompanying the Bronze Star, with which I was decorated upon leaving the Chinese Combat Command. I thought you might like to have it. Don't say anything, because the medal is sort of a Christmas surprise to the family. And Bethy, don't think ---although I'm sure you won't— that I'm even a little hero. I got it for being a "headquarters commando"!

Always with love,

Frosty

Frank Church was awarded the Bronze Star for his service in the U.S. Army.

CITATION

First Lieutenant (then Second Lieutenant) FRANK F. CHURCH, 0-1326316, Infantry, Army of the United States, is awarded the Bronze Star Medal for meritorious service during the period 3 May 1945 to 2 September 1945 as Officer in charge of the 42nd Order of Battle Team which was assigned to the G-2 Section, Chinese Combat Command. First Lieutenant CHURCH was delegated the responsibility of building up Order of Battle *files on Jap units south of the YANGTZE RIVER and west of the HANKOW-CANTON railway. These files, consisting of Japanese officers' names history, code names and numbers of Jap units, were well prepared and highly accurate, with the result that all Japanese movements were easily identified. In addition, First Lieutenant CHURCH materially expanded upon and improved reports and studies produced by the G-2 Section prior to his arrival. Periodically, he would publish a special study on individual Jap units wherein all available information on the unit was collated, collected, and evaluated. These studies were so well prepared that intelligence agencies, made requests for additional copies and language personnel in the field used the special studies as chief guides in interrogations. Aside from this Order of Battle work, First Lieutenant CHURCH was an inspiration to those who worked with him. He performed with wholehearted interest at all times, worked after hours continually, and sought constantly to improve upon his contributions. First Lieutenant CHURCH's meritorious service reflects great credit upon himself and the Armed Forces of the United States.*

OFFICIAL

Chinese Combat Command (Prov)

USF China Theater APO 627

"*Truman Promises Publicity on China; He Says Policy Instruction to Marshall as Envoy Will Be Available to Nation. Investigation is Assured.*"

N.Y. Times 11/30/1945

Shanghai, China
30 November 1945

Dearest Bethine,

News of Bob's [Wardwell] passing reached me only an hour ago.

Bob was more than a close friend—he was my brother. He was as part of my life in a way that none of my other friends can ever be. We grew up together, played together, fought together. We shared our boyhood with one another from the day we first met on the parking in front of my home. Bob called me "Foty" then, for he couldn't pronounce his "r's" and always forgot his "s's." How often he used to stand before the hall door and call me to come out to play, and how many were the times he would sit beside the bed when I was sick, upon finding that I couldn't come outdoors.

There were no secrets we didn't share. There were no little plans we didn't carefully lay in consultation. I remember the first half dollar we earned mowing a neighboring lawn, and how we invested it in a pair of toy binoculars, using them to peer out of the second-story window of a room I used upstairs. I remember our second purchase as well---drawing paper for our plans of a rocket ship we agreed to build for a trip to the moon! And I remember the time Bob and I frightened our playmates and annoyed the neighbors by alternately appearing in the dark as the "bat" dressed in a black cape and crepe-paper mask.

We once discovered, while hiking in the foothills, a cave dug deeply into the sand. That became our "hideout," the location of which we never divulged. By devious routes, we covered up our path when others tried to follow, and met in secret rendezvous before the cave, there to gloat about our success, and to plan "attacks" upon the valley below. We called our hideout "x4x."

The days of the "rubber-gun club" were among the happiest of my life. It was our club, Bob's and mine, for we summoned or dismissed the other members at our pleasure. I was the president, Bob the sergeant-at-arms. Ostensibly, we were elected, but I recall how often we found it necessary to stuff the ballot box in order to remain in power.

It's unnecessary for me to try and express my feeling toward Bob. You know of it perhaps better than anyone else. But all during the afternoon the memories have come crowding back to me---memories of our fire-engines, the toys we used to play with, of the electric train and how we devised new ways to test its power, of the family fire-works display on the night of the 4th, and the especially big chocolate ice cream soda Mother used to make for the two of us afterwards, of our fishing trip in the mountains when Dad, Mother and I caught many trout, but Bob caught only a minnow in four days of concentrated effort, of the days of swimming in the river, of the picnics, and parties, and dances, of the many happy times.

And among my closest memories, Bethy, are those of Bob we hold mutually. Although he dated many girls, you were always apart from the rest. He was deeply fond of you. I have always known that you were worthy of Bob's affection, but I believe now that I was not. He gave me more than I ever gave in return. And I didn't deserve half so much.

About a month ago, Bob sent me a snapshot of himself that I had asked him for. I'm sending it on to you. Please keep it for me. The picture is the latest I have of Bob, and it might be lost in the constant shuffle over here.

Tonight I'm very lonely. There is a vacuum that won't be filled. I want to see you so very much.

My love,

"Flash"

Senator Frank Church and David Tsu, who served as his Chinese interpreter during WWII, were reunited in Shanghai in 1979.

"From Tarawa to the Doorstep of Japan…At a time when the Pearl Harbor investigation committee is busy proving Mr. Roosevelt forced the Japs to attack us…"

N.Y. Times 12/9/1945

Shanghai, China
9 December 1945

Dear Bethy,

It is strange to watch the Christmas Season approach with none of the traditional trappings to clothe it. If it were not for the fact that I often think of how wonderful it would be to spend Christmas at home, the whole holiday period might pass with only the passing realization that it had come and gone. There is little in Shanghai to remind one of the Christmas spirit. [In 1979, Frank Church was reunited with his WWII Chinese interpreter in Shanghai].

Yes it is true that Shanghai is a fabulous, turbulent, polyglot and exciting city. It is equally true that Shanghai is hard, and shameless, selfish, and mercenary. No visit to the Orient could be complete without becoming acquainted with this city, and without living among its imponderable people. Built and administered largely by the British, Shanghai has now been returned to the Chinese, who have yet to demonstrate the ability to run a modern city. The fortune of war spared Shanghai from much damage. Outside of a few bombings along the waterfront, the city is wholly intact. The occupation, however, leaves its mark in the form of certain deficiencies. The Japanese stripped the principal buildings of radiators early in the war, the result being that we are now largely without heat. At about the same time, the most modern buses and the best automobiles were also confiscated by the Japanese with the intent to ship the loot to Japan. Many weeks were required to collect all those vehicles, to properly service them, and to load them aboard two transport ships for the voyage. Both ships sailed down the river with their cargo, and both ships were sunk at the mouth of the open sea. Because of the Japanese control of rental rates during the occupation, a control that reduced rents to almost nothing, thus helping to improve the popularity of the administration, and, at the same time render property almost worthless, the buildings everywhere are in a state of disrepair. Such is the state of physical damage the war inflicted upon Shanghai. A flesh wound, no more.

The coming of peace and the return of the Chungking government, ironically enough, have served to aggravate more serious problems. Inflation, bad enough during the war, has become progressively worse during the past three months. The housing shortage is acute as a consequence of the arrival of large numbers of Chinese and American troops. The municipal government is practically impotent, and akin to its big brother, the national government, notoriously corrupt. It seems capable of nothing other than throwing its weight around by imposing exorbitant taxes and enforcing annoying curfews. Chiang is fast losing prestige among the people.

But these are questions too complex to expound upon at the moment. Better to turn to more personal things.

I am living at the Hamilton House, one of many hotels taken over by the Army, with my old friend, Eley, and another Michigan graduate, Dave… We are quite comfortable, having procured an electric heater by a great stroke of luck, and being equipped with a kitchen, living room, bedroom and bath. With some ease, it is possible to cook up a meal, or to serve tea after the British fashion in the afternoon, or to modestly entertain in the evening. This is all wonderfully different from the interior days.

Among the people I have met here in Shanghai, the Sulkes are by far the most interesting. Mr. Sulke is a German Jew, formerly a successful and prominent businessman in the Reich, who was forced to leave that country in 1939. He married a German Aryan just before leaving, bringing her with him to Shanghai. He is now in business with two Chinese partners, and appears to be doing well once again. A person of the most amazing mental agility, …. has learned to speak both English and Chinese since his arrival here, and has many an interesting story to tell regarding his experiences in Germany as well as those he has encountered in business with the Chinese. He is also very much interested in America, and constantly astonishes me with his knowledge of American history and contemporary politics. They have been very good to me. I find that getting back to the surroundings of a family home is powerful tonic, and that sharing company with the …. provides refreshing relief from the hum-drum character of Army life. It will be something to have someone with whom to celebrate Christmas.

I don't expect to be homeward bound for at least another two months. Nothing is so awkward for the Army as demobilization, and plans for a permanent military mission over here have served to interfere with the deactivation of the theater. Until I can manage to get out on points---and I have only 51---or to get declared surplus at a time when there is no longer danger of reassignment, I'll have to stick it out.

Your Christmas present is just a gesture, and I'm not at all satisfied with what I was able to send. However, Bethy, I have been able to get some Japanese things that I like muchly, and will either send them through the mail or bring them home with me when I come, whichever you prefer. Several are quite lovely, I think, choice tributes to a wonderful gal----

Always with love,

Frosty, Frosty, Frosty

p.s. The two extra signatures are for the two letters I missed signing.

"If there is one truth that should have been impressed upon us the last few years it is that citizenship in a democracy involves duties as well as rights. To have good government we must share in the burdens of governing. To maintain our liberties we must be willing to defend them. It was not enough to wish for peace; we had to fight for it"

N.Y. Times 12/19/1945

Shanghai, China
19 December 1945

Dearest Bethy,

It is bright and cheerful in Shanghai this afternoon. After two days of bitterly cold weather, the sun has put the clouds to flight, and the winds are still. I am seated at my stenographer's desk, in an empty office, thinking of Christmas and you. Outside, the streets are teeming. Rickshaws and pedicabs, trucks and jeeps, passenger cars of every conceivable foreign and American make, mix with hundreds of pedestrians. Nothing can compare, in terms of activity and confusion, with a crowded Shanghai street scene. I have just returned from a tiffin engagement with some Chinese acquaintances. Mr. Sulke whom I mentioned in a recent letter, an interesting old British sea captain, who made his living for more than thirty years in the coastal trade, and who has just been released from an internment camp, and several other Chinese businessmen. We had Swatow food, something new for me, all of which was well prepared, while the final dish was so unusual in its preparation and service that it warrants mention here. First of all, we were brought half a dozen plates containing thin slices of raw meat, slips of chicken liver, kidney, gizzard, slices of beef and pork. Next, a charcoal burner was placed in the middle of the table filled with boiling chicken broth. The host then proceeds to cook the parcels of meat in the broth, a little ceremony that requires no more than three or four minutes. The guests, in the meantime, prepare their own sauce in separate bowls, beginning with a raw egg, and mixing in broth and wine to taste. Once this is accomplished, everybody dips into the boiling soup with his chopsticks, taking out whatever he most prefers, covers it with the sauce he has prepared, and happily concerns himself with the business of eating. A thoroughly delightful proceeding. As I have said before, Bethy, the art of eating is one of China's chief attributes.

I received a letter from Mother this morning that serves to emphasize the effect of a badly misdirected War Department publicity campaign. She enclosed a clipping, which must have appeared in the Statesman, to the effect that all high point servicemen, plus all others who will be surplus to the China Theater needs, will be on their way home by the 10th of December. Such is not only untrue but it is also the reason that so many families in the States are now anticipating arrivals that do not materialize. Mother said that she was even preparing my room for me. Bethy, I don't know how to tell Mother that it will be several more months before I can expect to get home. I have already mentioned the fact in a letter posted last week, and certainly I would have done so less bluntly had I received this letter beforehand. As things now stand, I can't expect to get away before sometime in late February or early March, and perhaps even later than that.

Shanghai is preparing for a holiday next Saturday. The Generalissimo is expected to visit the city, probably in connection with greeting General Marshall. Incidentally, I learned this afternoon that Christmas is a holiday in China since it happens to be the anniversary of Chiang's release by the Communists in the notorious kidnapping episode of many years ago. That was a mistake the Communists have yet to recover from!

In my association with new friends here in Shanghai, and partly as the result of my own experience in China, I have learned a number of interesting stories that reveal, to an appreciable extent, the character of Chinese government, and the methods, time-honored and inherent, to be found both in business and in politics. Several of these are stories I should like to remember, but the details soon fade away and are forgotten. If I can find the time, Bethy, and if you would be interested, I would like to write up a few of the better ones, and send them on to you. This proposition is in fact a safeguard. In those moments when, out of loss of memory or good sense, I feel unreasonably sympathetic toward the Chinese, I can turn to these accounts for correction. At least, it's a suggestion.

What kind of sales girl do you make, Bethy? Are you an asset or a liability? You tell me that you don't make enough to even cover your Christmas expenses! That means you are either very poorly paid, or that your expenses are extravagant, and I suspect the latter is the case. What in the world are you going to do, Bethy, when you have to live on twenty-five dollars a week?

I don't seem to have said very much, and the office is getting dark. Gosh, I wish we could celebrate New Year's together! Will you settle for the Easter Parade?

Love muchly,

Frosty

[*Poem attached to two rosewood statues Frank Church sent from China to Bethine for Christmas 1945*]

It Must Be Admitted

(Though hardly a Christmas thought)

Growing handsome growing old

Is the promise, I am told,

Of couples who are bound

In honest love----------------

But this lady and this gent,

In the box that I have sent,

Must certainly have fought and

Sinned as well,

For the old man looks the measure

Of his wife's sardonic pleasure,

As she contemplates their rendezvous

In Hell!

So let this be a warning,

To the marriages now forming,

In proof that age will bear a message clear,

And that one's radiant complexion

Is in fact a true reflection

Of new happiness in each succeeding year.

Dear Frosty,

[first portion of letter missing]

It will be interesting and will stop gap 'til January. After that I shall decide on a civil service or some other type of job, probably in New York or Washington, D.C. Jean and Glen have an apartment in N.Y. Barbie and Gusty are both in Washington.

I bought your Christmas present today. I'll have a personal Christmas when you get home. I do wish you could have it Christmas, but hurry and get it, right here.

Your second gift came, and it is fascinating me, but I promise I'll wait for both 'til Christmas.

For now, good night.

Love, Bethy

"In the Nation on the Verge of Historic Change. The ethical concept that men are brothers and peace is the heritage of men of goodwill, which the advent of Christmas illuminates for the western world, has throughout history gained little more than lip service..."

N.Y. Times 12/25/1945

China
Christmas, 1945

Dearest Bethy,

People who have been in the Orient often prove that fact with the fans they've purchased there. This one is from Hangchow, the city most famous for its fans. Bethy, I don't know to what possible use you can put it, but is bright and colorful, and fragrant with the heavy scent of sandalwood.

It's just a little gift, but I liked it, and thought you might like to have it.

Merry Tidings,

Frank

It Was with the Best Intention---

I was looking for some silk one day,

To make a summer dress for May,

Of course I thought of you

In a frock of gold-buff hue,

And I seized upon the silk and made away.

But Bethy, I'm sad to say,

That I found to my dismay,

Upon readying this parcel for the mail,

That the silk had frayed and soiled,

And I fear that it is spoiled,

For it looks the last sad remnant of a gale!

Frosty

OFFICE OF HEADQUARTERS

COMMANDANT USF CT

APO 971

15 Jan 1946

SUBJECT: Officers for Duty in the Military Intelligence Service

TO: War Department General Staff

               Military Intelligence Division

               Attn: Director of Administration

1. This is in reply to your letter of 18 December 1945 Regarding candidates recommended for the Military Intelligence Service. I very much appreciate having been included in the List of prospective candidates, but I must advise you that it is my intention to return to civilian life.

2. Although I would have interest in joining a reserve Corps of intelligence officers, your specification that only Regular Army Officers or those intending to remain in the regular establishment are eligible for assignment automatically disqualifies me for consideration.

FRANK F. CHURCH

1st Lt. Inf.,

0-1326316

Having turned down a military appointment after WWII, Church returned to Stanford University in 1946 to complete his undergraduate education using his American Legion scholarship and his G.I. benefits.

"Oneworld' Motif of Assembly Room; "World of Tomorrow' Provides Street Names for United Nations...."

N.Y. Times 9/24/1946

Stanford, CA
24 September 1946

My Darling,

I am in the midst of a hectic day---registration day. The lines have a character of unendingness, while the "quad" looks very much like the main lobby of Grand Central at noon. This place was never meant for seven thousand students.

My own situation is the best I could possibly hope for. Dave... and I share a comfortable room up on the third deck of the Theta Xi house, a room made especially attractive by the fact that Dave...owns a sizeable library, housed in three separate bookcases, some fifty albums of records, an excellent Victrola, a radio, a cabinet, a large lamp, and one of the easiest of easy chairs. All of this leaves just enough room for my scanty property, and provides us with an exceedingly cozy, academic-appearing refuge. I have never felt properly attuned to college in the barren, cell-like cubicles of Encina Hall. Now, for the first time, I feel surrounded by a comforting, fitting environment. I say "fitting"--- in the hope that it will prove conducive to study, although I suspect that I'll be easily drawn away by the beckon of the records and the books.

Our trip down was a funny one in many ways. Phyllis and Ginny, coming from hardy pioneer stock, thought it would be wonderful ---as well as less expensive---to spend the night under the pines in the high Sierras! Carl and I tried to talk them out of it, but they were determined, and we were guests, and so the night was spent at a height of nearly 8,000 feet---Carl and I huddled in the trunk---Phyllis and Ginny beneath a thick stack of blankets under the pines. We put up at about midnight, anticipating a sudden disillusionment. We weren't to wait long. At about two in the morning, Phyllis came chattering out from beneath her blankets, frozen to the point of incoherence. It took until seven in the morning to warm her up. We had to immediately get underway, place her between the two of us in the front seat, and fill her with hot coffee at intervals until the sun arose to take over the job.

The course I planned to take I managed to put through. It will be a very heavy load. I'll let you know how it develops.

Bethy, I miss you. Write to me often and soon. The address is: Theta Xi, Stanford University, Calif.

I'll be waiting for your letters, waiting to hear of your doings, your thoughts, and your plans; I'll be waiting to see you again, waiting for Christmas when I can be with you, when I can tell that

I love you,

Frosty

"Julliard Enrolls 1,800; Record Matriculation Includes 500 Veterans Under G.I. Bill."

N.Y. Times 9/29/1946

Stanford, CA
29 Sept. 1946

My Darling Bethy,

Your letter was wonderful. I was glad to hear that, as you put it you had lost your wisdom, and that you were progressing through the second and third rows on the typewriter. I was amused, though not surprised, that you failed to appreciate the quickened interest displayed by Pancho's friend, and I will think that .... and I are going to become fast friends. I hope I have an alliance in the opposing camp, although, if necessary, I'm willing to carry on the battle alone.

I just read your joke to Dave who paused long enough from his law pursuits to listen. Dave asked me to tell you that he is now studying cases where the defendants are indicted for eavesdropping, and, what's more, convicted. This is the best answer I can give you.

The big event for the weekend past down here was the opening of the football season with a stampede over Idaho to the tune of 45 to 0. I found myself watching the debacle with mixed feelings, wishing that Idaho would refrain from condemning itself to the axe block in so public a way. Such were my sentiments at least during the first half of the game. Then I learned that Wade back in Moscow, apparently carried completely away in the wild grip of campus hysteria, was betting 5 to 1 on Idaho! I must confess that I enjoyed the second half of the game tremendously.

It's swell to be back once more with Dave, and to become involved in his complicated love affairs. During one of his sojourns in this connection---this time during an afternoon in Berkeley

---I happened to step into a very surprising co-incidence. I had left the house, which was located near the top of the hill above Berkeley, and was idling up the sidewalk humming to myself in a state of pseudo-consciousness when I happened to run into an old acquaintance of mine whom I had known in the Orient. He lived nearby, was married to a Stanford girl (this, I believe is his fourth marriage!), and was renting his house, having moved into the cottage in the rear of the garden, to a Major Tussman, that is formerly, whom I had worked under for several months in Kunming. They were both connected with Cal---which is not surprising since few aren't nowadays---Jim in attendance there, and Tussman on the faculty.

I should like to tell you something of recent developments, Bethy, but I must close in order to make class. Having been conditioned during the Summer for nine o'clocks, I slept through my eight o'clock this morning, was late to my nine o'clock, whereupon my pen went dry, and I was forced to copy all the notes afterwards. You see, I'm just a might foggy.

Several of us are laying quiet plans to escape the fraternity, and take over a hunting lodge off campus. This has many advantages, the details of which I'll deal with later.

Christmas will be fun, great fun. My love, Frosty.

"U.N. Delegations Chosen."

N.Y. Times 10/7/1946

[In 1967, Senator Frank Church served as the Senate delegate to the United Nations in NY]

Stanford University
October 7, 1946

Darling,

Just a note to let you know I'm thinking of you. It's funny that I should during the course of the day, think of so many different things to write you about, and then to find, upon sitting down with pen in hand, that I have either forgotten them, or that they seem unimportant. The only important matter it seems, is you. This, as you might suspect, is not at all rational---and I have always prided myself by fostering the illusion that I'm a purely rational guy---but it is a fact nonetheless.

Dave and I spent yesterday afternoon on the beach at Santa Cruz. It was something of a novelty for me since I've only the scantiest acquaintance with the breakers, the even, sandy beaches, and the cold, foaming, sparkling waters of the surf. I had a wonderful time running along near the water's edge, tumbling the sand, riding the waves into the shore, and generally behaving like a care-free and exuberant puppy dog. I proved to myself that I had not yet grown so old as to have lost the capacity for play, even though at the expense of shocking several sedate couples who had apparently come to the beach on doctor's orders, and who looked to be resenting each minute.

Bethy, did I tell you?

I love you,

Frosty

"Dewey Salutes China's Republic."

N.Y. Times 10/14/1946

Stanford
October 14, 1946

Darling,

It's midnight. I've spent the evening over some damned provoking accounting papers which left me in no mood to attempt a letter. But then one is due.

I've had a hell of a time settling down to study. I don't know why, but it's actually been harder at the beginning of this term than it was last summer. I find myself turning more and more to methods of escape, to the point of running errands, straightening the room, cleaning out my desk, talking with Dave or with Bay, skipping out for a beer, listening by the hour to records in the room, going downstairs for a coke, shooting a game of pool, or simply falling asleep in a chair, all in a seemingly incurable effort to avoid studying. This carries over into frequent trips to the city, and great motor expeditions south to Los Angeles, an absolute inability to get up in the morning in time for my eight o'clock, as well as an alarming weakness for falling fast asleep at my nine o'clocks. In short, McGee, I'm shot. I have really never been so loathe to exact at least a semblance of self-discipline. But it's a glorious anarchy. Maybe the pressure of poor grades will force me to get down to serious study soon. Still, the thought of it is deadening.

Bethy, since I got your last letter, I've been thinking about the dinner party you mentioned at my place. Wasn't it a funny assortment? I mean Uncle Bern and his big kid ways, the Admiral and his gruff, bluff sea stories, Aunt Marion and her sophisticated, charming, but perceptibly superior manner, Eva with her strict sense of propriety, Dad with his propensity for getting involved in awkward political controversy, your father with his frank and winning friendliness of the best Western tradition, Iva who undoubtedly talked about the doings of Barbara and Patty, your mother, who may well have questioned the correctness of the whole affair considering things as they now stand, and my mother, who must have ushered people about and worked madly in the kitchen to prepare the food and get it properly served. All of this, and you with a bad head cold. I can't help but believe that the evening must have had its funnier aspects. Tell me, did Albert stay sober? Did he try to force a whole platter of drinks on the Judge? Or did you make discreet arrangements to prevent anything of that sort beforehand? I wish I had been there, but then perhaps I would have been the last straw---which is entirely possible.

Your bedroom sounds enchanting. I have never seen nor heard about anything quite like it before. How has it turned out, Bethy? What's the effect anyway?

Bay and I took Dave's car last Thursday and drove south for the Stanford-U.C.L.A. football game. We spent the night in Santa Barbara, where Bay's mother presides in a fabulous ranch house, seated on the high slopes of the mountains behind and above the city, overlooking the ocean. The ranch extends over four thousand acres of orchard and mountain side, while the house itself, a rambling Californian place, sets like a rich plum in a foliaged court. I was completely swept away by the place. They had a natural, circular pool accessible by road above the ranch house, so situated that it was at once wholly isolated and private, and at the same time open to the most breathtaking view of the mountains immediately above, of the sweep of orchards immediately below, of the city, and of the sea reaching out to the horizon. Santa Barbara has held fast to a pseudo-feudal order; the great manor houses rise above each separate domain, and the owners, the nobility, live on a rich and expansive scale.

We spent Friday night in North Hollywood at the home of a guy called [Tommy] Rafferty. Rafferty plays character roles in the movies. He last appeared in The Big Sleep as the kid affiliate of the racketeer, the guy who shot six times at Humphrey Bogart and missed him with every shot, something I couldn't quite forgive him for. Dave came down on the plane Saturday. We saw the game, partied that evening, and enjoyed a very pleasant trip back to Stanford on Sunday.

As for news, Bethy, there is little else at the moment. I'm scheduled to participate with two others on a panel to appear before the International Club next Sunday. The subject has to do with the virtues and defects of American colleges, but I agreed to take part in spite of the subject, and all because they promise a Mexican dinner. The call of Mexico snaps me to action anywhere.

Carl ran for ExCom representative from the "Row." He was one of two elected yesterday which make him a mighty happy man today. He'll make a fine representative on the committee.

My letters never seem to be as successful as yours. And you, McGee, seem to be following the policy of tit-for-tat, one letter to me for one letter to you which is eminently fair, but then I don't hear from you as often as I'd like.

You can imagine how late it is by now. I was so tired when I began this letter that I missed the date by three days in the letterhead, all of which may indicate that I am now in a state of quasi-collapse. Let me crawl off to bed, to picture you, the stern Goddess on Olympus, who is going to anchor me firmly and unshakably to the pillars of propriety.

Don't do that to me please!

I love you, Frosty

"Birthday of Atomic Era Dec. 2, 1942, Army Rules."

N.Y. Times 10/26/1946

Stanford University
26 October 1946

My Darling,

All evening I've been in a Parisian mood. I've been thinking of gaiety and laughter, of broad avenues and sidewalk cafes. Rich Burgundy and fragrant Sauterne wines have loomed up all through the evening, while I've watched, in fancy, an unending procession of tempting French dishes pass by. And as my wild day dreaming brought us together in Paris, convincing me that two young people never really live without a year in France, I was obliged to sit home at the desk doing accounting problems! What can be more frustrating, Bethy, than having to check trial balances and prepare [illegible] statements of "Profits and Loss" while thinking of Paris in the early Spring. What awful torture!

There's been a most unusual addition to our room since I last wrote. You'd never guess what it is. At the same time, I can't possibly describe it. The best I can do is name it. We now boast a surrealist door. One of Bay's good friends is an artist who is both engrossed in, and remarkably adept at, surrealist painting. He prepared a striking design for the door to the room, and painted it in rich colors. We managed to sneak it through before the rest of the house found out about it. The interior decoration committee, which presently entertains some melancholy plan to repaint all the rooms a uniform brown, was a bit perturbed by the door. Without doubt, it constitutes an alarming departure from the best traditions of the fraternity. But by the time the committee had gotten around to proposing "a uniform brown" the door was a fait accompli. So we are now the proud possessors of the first and, without doubt, the only surrealist door that is apt to appear on the Stanford campus.

First you enclose a traffic ticket and then you smash up the car. Bethy, let's not allow vanity to interfere with wearing those glasses when you drive. Are you teaching English at the college, or collecting papers? Tell me about these things.

I am planning to open up with all guns firing next Wednesday afternoon in an address on China. The School of Education asked me to an assembly in the education auditorium where I'm to give an hour's lecture of the current Chinese situation. The address I plan to give is likely to prove quite controversial. If I'm run out of Stanford, will you still marry me?

My love always,

Frosty

"Back Peace Policy, Eisenhower Urges; The Emperor Talks with the Children of Japan."

N.Y. Times 11/2/1946

Stanford University
November 2, 1946

My Darling,

The best in convention dictates that one should not write his fiancé on the typewriter, and I agree. But this is a very special typewriter. I was given this typewriter at about the time I first met you, when you came down from Idaho Falls to participate in the Student Body Officers' Convention. Thus, I cannot help but feel that I'm punching sympathetic keys. Yes, this is a very special typewriter; it's an old friend of yours.

I think you would have been happy with me Wednesday, Bethy. As you know, I had been anxious for the chance to strike out against Chiang's China for a long time. The opportunity to do so on a somewhat larger scale than conversationally in the living room of a parlor pink came in the form of an invitation from the School of Education here to address an assembly in the Education Auditorium. I decided to go at it in a no-holds barred fashion, and gave an hour's talk that created quite a sensation among those present. It was something of a teapot tempest, the Daily carrying only a brief announcement of the talk beforehand, and nothing thereafter, but the people who were there were at once astonished and enthusiastic. I have a raincheck for a return engagement, in addition to a request from the Graduate School of Business to take part on a panel discussion dealing with economic affairs in the Orient, plus an invitation to submit to a question-answer session in one of the Chinese history classes here. So you can see that the talk caused quite a stir. I really enjoyed giving it. Of course I was fortunate in having a liberally-minded group to speak to. It occurred to me later that if I were to give substantially the same talk to a large, representative group in Boise, the stuffy Statesman would roar in righteous anger for days, and the Legion protégé would become the "menace of Franklin Street." [*The Church family home at 10th and Franklin Streets in Boise*]

I'm also going to have a chance to take a crack at the proposed six-month draft on a national hook-up next Friday, November 8th. There will be four of us in a panel discussion on the American School Hour, sponsored, I believe, by the American Economic Foundation. The program is scheduled to be covered by "Pic Magazine" so if you don't manage to pick it up on the radio, you may later get a coverage of it there. I have no idea how it will pan out, but it ought to prove interesting.

This letter has been all about me, Bethy. Apologies are in order. I received your last letter, and, as a result, am increasingly excited over prospects for Mexico. Christmas will be along soon. Let's make the most of it.

All my love,

Frosty

"Vandenberg Vows Biparty Aid to U.N.; Delegates Applaud Pledge of Continued U.S. Faith in the Organization as Peace Aim."

N.Y. Times 11/9/1946

Stanford
November 9, 1946

My Darling,

Time for a letter, and a Saturday morning in which to write it. Bethy, you may say "Time for a letter is right!," but I turned in idle moments (of which there were few) during the week to Schopenhauer's "Studies in Pessimism," finding there his essay, "On Women"—a withering attack upon the sex from which I've absolved you, Bethy, as a particular exception to the general rule. Schopenhauer concedes only that "Without women the beginning of our life would be helpless; the middle, devoid of pleasure; and the end, of consolation." Of course, I need to grant that too.

I wasn't drunk when I last wrote, Bethy. Actually, I was just in my usual daze. Someday I expect to send a letter meant for you to an old girlfriend, but I hope never to blunder so badly as to reverse that kind of mistake. What a terrible mishap that would be!

But you captured the mood masterfully in:

Safe upon the solid rock

> the ugly houses stand
>
> Come and see my shining palace
>
> Built upon the sand.

Let's never live in an "ugly house," Bethy. I'm confident we never will.

Yes, Bethy, let's do have an announcement during the Christmas holidays. Would you like a dinner party for the occasion with just selected friends? It makes no difference to me however you may want to handle it.

If we must go to the Judges' formal dinner, o.k., but I don't have any formal clothing, and might be able to beg off on that account.

Oh yes, the radio program went off without any major fumble yesterday afternoon. The whole proceeding had been misrepresented to us, however, only the first part of the program —consisting of a pro & con address from the East---being nationwide, while the latter half, the panel discussion, was made up of a number of different panel groups from representative universities, broadcasting regionally. Our own part went on the air from the Columbia station in San Jose.

In about the middle of the week Carl made the team for the program which made our collective opposition to the six month draft unanimous. We simply took turns at the microphone condemning the proposal.

I took in the "Duchess of Malfi" last night at San Jose. It was one of the best class-produced, that is, college student performances I've seen.

Needless to mention, Bethy, Stanford is still in an orgy of exuberance over the Republican landslide. Ticker tape falls over Wall Street, the bankers embrace one another on the sidewalks, Hoover, proving himself long since senile, proclaims a victory for the "Right," and Stanford wildly applauds. I wonder how I ever chose from my university such a pesthole of reaction.

Naturally, the boys have good reasons to celebrate. One guy I know—he sports a new Cadillac on campus—told me that the time was now at hand for his father to make his fair cut. He expects to be sporting three Cadillacs by next Spring.

Well, the boom will come even more furiously. We'll swell and swell, and bloat and burst, and you and I will be clapped flat in the crash. Ah well, chasing ambulances may prove varied and interesting. All kinds of pretty girls get into awkward accidents!

Bethy, I love you,

Frosty

p.s. I have both name and address right this time. Gotta keep things straight.

"Atom Bombs Held Cheap, Plentiful; the Emergency Committee of Atomic Scientists Meets"

N.Y. Times 11/18/1946

Stanford
November 18, 1946

Bethy Darling,

As I read your letter, I pictured you lounging on the couch before the fireplace fondling the cat (among your few weaknesses is your imponderable fondness for cats), and busily writing away on the events of the past week.

I wish I had been in your English class at the college. What a heckler you would have had on your hands. From what you say, however, I think the class must have been quite a success.

It sounds to me as if all the people on the "right" (socially "right") side of the tracks---available in the area, with Southwest Idaho thrown in for good measure—are to be invited to the announcement tea. What are you going to do, block off three blocks on Main Street for the occasion?

My own conception of the affair had been quite different. I thought it would be fitting to hold a stag chug-a-lug party down at the Challenger, with you hidden in great card board cake in the middle of the room. At the moment I made the announcement---late in the evening---you would break forth from the cake in a shower of frosting, and we all throw beer bottles. The next morning pictures in the Statesman would naturally be of me, standing with Samurai sword in hand, about ready to slice the cake. This would not only be an original form, but it would also be symbolic of the coming event. I can see the story now:

"Bethine Clark, about to be released by the sword of passion from the frosted confinement of maiden life."

Actually, though, the only people---since you limit me to the opposite sex—whom I might suggest for the tea would be those few old flames of mine who still remain unmarried. Since they might cause quite a fuss (you know how frustrated women behave), perhaps it's best to leave them uninvited. Besides, including them would swell the total numbers so that you would probably have to hold the affair in the High School Gymnasium! After all, you're preparing for only a modest three hundred. Idaho apparently hasn't graduated into the "400 "category.

The formal, candle light dinner sounds swell. I would like to suggest two fellows you didn't mention, Wade …., and Don….. Would the including of them and their dates make the party unwieldy? If Carl and Stan come, as they must, then I think Wade and Don should be included as well.

Darling, I have a wonderful present for you---several in fact---for Christmas. But I'll need some suggestions on what to get your mother and father. As for me, thanks for asking. A few of the gifts I would most appreciate might include one among the following possibilities:

(1) A Ronson cigarette lighter.

(2) A good anthology of English poetry

(3) Shoe, brown sport or dress, size about 10B, I think.

(4) White dress shirts

(5) A suitcase

I expect just a token present from you, a handkerchief perhaps, but you might pass the word on to Mother and Dad about the list suggestions. Nothing like making Christmas practical.

You mentioned that our transportation problem was solved. That's wonderful news. What is the detailed answer?

This has turned into a lengthy letter, Darling, one filled with nonsense and banter. What I wanted to write is that I love you, and that I'm anxiously waiting out these few remaining weeks until Christmas. Then we'll celebrate gloriously, festively together.

All my love,

Frosty

"French to Discuss Indo-Chinese Reds. While the Communists claim the Premiership of the new Government, the Cabinet is expected to discuss tomorrow the fighting between French forces in Haiphong, Indo-China, and troops of the Communist leader there, Ho Chi Minh."

N.Y. Times 11/27/1946

Stanford University
November 27, 1946

Bethy, M'Darlin,

Thanksgiving vacation is here marking the prelude to the final session of the quarter. Will we have snow for Christmas? Let's have Christmas with all the tinsel and trimming, Bethy. Order snow for me, will you? And we'll shop together for the family presents, and we'll trim the two trees together, and hang the wreaths and mistletoe, and mix the eggnogs, and keep a bright fire in the hearth, crackling into the night. And because happiness is contagious, we'll make everyone wondrously happy by our example. It will be an unforgettable Christmas.

I was planning a trip South to Los Angeles as late as this morning. But then I took count of my finances, and skeptically risked a look at a long list of neglected assignments, and decided to stay here over the vacation period. Only one more week of classes remain, and then a week of finals, and then I'll be back again to see you.

The past week has been chocked full of activities. There was the Big Game with Cal last Saturday which ended happily with a 25 to 6 victory for Stanford. The resumption of the old tradition exploded with all its customary color and excitement. The Berkeley campus was in circus attire, with houses draped in bunting, mock-ups, and game slogans. One of the best I recall appeared on one of the sorority houses. It read:

How're we gonna keep em down on "the farm,"

After they've seen U.C.

That night, Bluf and Brenchley and I took in Laurence Oliver's presentation of Henry V in the city. If you haven't seen it, Bethy, it's wonderful. It's the first real artistic achievement that I've seen on the screen. All through the picture I kept asking myself how it could possibly have been improved upon. It's an emphatic "must," Bethy.

I've also managed, after a wait of six years or more, to see "Life with Father." I enjoyed it a great deal. While we're on the subject of plays and pictures, there is another that warrants special mention. "Caesar and Cleopatra" is showing on the coast now. It is an extravaganza in technicolor with too much mimicry of Hollywood technique, but the character portrayals of Caesar and Cleopatra are superb. The acting is brilliant, and Shaw's dialogue masterful. Perhaps the picture will show in Boise during the holidays. It if does, providing you haven't seen it already, we'll have to take it in one evening.

I've always prided myself, Bethy, in my unequaled fairness in these matters of compatibility. The answer to the question you propose is quite simple, to wit:

(1) If I want to ride on the roller coaster, we do so.

(2) If you want to ride on the roller coaster, you may.

Is there any chance that you can keep your friends from the bottle at our wedding, dear? If so, you have better discipline among them than I have among my California buddies. For that matter, you had better concentrate upon your future husband. Going through an affair of this kind soberly is likely to lead to serious psychological repercussion. As for my close friends here, Baker tells me that he plans to appear with two stunning chorus girls from San Francisco, and Bluf insists that his wedding present shall consist of a case of champagne. This is hardly the best Puritan form.

Bethy, I'll write your father tonight, and thank him for the article. It was an interesting account of present-day opportunities for the prospective lawyer, and I appreciated it a lot.

The best that can be said for Bill.... is that he knows a good woman when he sees one.

Darling, I love you,

Frosty

"Chiang Renews Bid to Reds for Peace; Aide Invites Parley on End of Fighting and Revamping of Government Set-Up."

N.Y. Times 1/10/1947

January 10, 1947

Darling,

I have been away from my typewriter for a month, and subjected to the tedium of handwriting the whole while, so now I plan to make up for lost time, since the problem is that of lack of time, and use it for this letter.

What is there, Darling, of new news? Well, Carl pinned Spicer [Carolyn Spice Burke] yesterday, having to buy the pin to the tune of fifty dollars. This puts C.B. badly in debt, a setback he sees little promise of overcoming before the quarter is out. He tells me

—and I agree—that it is the most inexpensive way he can think of for getting almost engaged. The ring he says will come later, much later.

Dave came floating back to school in high spirits. He seems to be in the best psychological health, at least for the present. As I mentioned before, I can't quite believe that he will actually marry next summer—too much time for too much water under the bridge. He still, naturally, runs in robust emotional cycles (I think the psychologist would diagnose his case as being very mildly that of a manic-depressive), and each time he completes a cycle he comes around again on a new vehicle. The latest is his enthusiasm for his return to pre-medical studies. He told me this morning that his project of the quarter was an exhaustive research on the anterior lobe of the pituitary gland: such is Bluford's charm.

Brenchley and I are the only two of the group who remain this quarter in the house. We live in a kind of splendid, though undeclared, isolation, spending our social hours largely in the world beyond. And the "world beyond" seems to hold much of interest in the coming months.

Oh, yes Darling. If you haven't read my letter home, then I should mention that Dr. Thompson, who invited me to address his Rotary Club meeting just before the holidays—you'll remember our discussion on that subject—was kind enough to send a carton of cigarettes to me, and a package , but will mail it on when I post this letter tomorrow.

Sulke writes that he may be in this country next summer, perhaps in time for the wedding. Dave says that he has fallen in love with you through my descriptions, and wants eagerly to meet you; Baker says that the course he's taking in Buddhism is "wonderful in a terrible sort of way;" Andy painted the door of all doors for Chester in Oceana over the holidays; that's the news from the peninsula. The only other news is that I love you and

Miss you,

Frosty

"Only Defense Head Will Be in Cabinet in Army-Navy Plan; Secretaries of War, Navy, Air Will Not Get Such Status but May Consult the President."

N.Y. Times 1/18/1947

```
                                            Stanford
                                    January 18, 1947
```

Dearest,

You wrote a wow of a business letter. I was so impressed in fact that I decided to buy a half-ownership in "The Clark Company," surmounting the letterhead. Do you think you could arrange to consummate the deal in about the middle of next June? I should have my own affairs in good order by that time.

Of course, as philosophy goes, I think it wise to begin at the beginning too. It is possible to erect ivory palaces upon the sand, but extremely difficult to find a philosophical adjustment with no foundation to raise it upon. Do I sound like Helen?

Darling, if you want to write damn in a letter to me, write damn. D---is hard to locate in a dictionary, and I might be badly misled. After all, you and I are old friends, and we shouldn't let a few solid, forthright words dash between us that way.

I hope your mom is feeling better, Bethy, and that the cold you mentioned has passed her by. Give them both my love, together with my warmest good wishes on their anniversary. I don't know of two happier people.

My congratulations are in order for Chase as well in the matter of Juvenile Delinquency. His views, I think, are the right ones on the subject, and it's swell that he has the chance to press for them on a national scale.

Go to it, Darling! I expect that you will be playing very ably when I see you next---and next time, you know, is for good. And the typing---well, your letter showed all kinds of improvement there, and I'm happy to hear that you determined to finish the "Razor's Edge."

The I.F. announcement, at least, had fewer errors than the one in the Statesman, although there seem to be some kind of cruel conspiracy to "betroth" us. I have included the clipping in the envelope for your safekeeping.

You closed your last letter with a reference to "Bloomer Girl," which reminds me that Dave received his record album of "Finnian's Rainbow," Harburg's latest Broadway show. I listened to the music yesterday. It's good, but I don't think up to standard. Another man has written the music, and I think you're right about

Arlen's work in the other two hits. This is inclined to be a little weighty, with less freshness and spontaneity. However, there are a couple of very clever songs, one of which goes: "If I'm not near the girl I love, then I love the girl I'm near." The other line, the best you'll agree, goes: "Follow the fellow who follows a dream."

Darling, the debate against California went remarkably well. Don't ask me why! It remains a mystery why it didn't prove an awful debacle. The question you may remember was, Resolved: that Federal control over labor unions should be increased, a question which is heavily weighted in favor of the affirmative at the present time. I could argue the negative in good faith, since I support it in principle, but there are without a doubt certain union abuses which could be tempered through appropriate legislation, and the evidence of this is overwhelming. Well, as you know, we had the negative. What was worse, neither Dow nor I had even begun to prepare when the debate was upon us. As I recall it now, these are the scenes that come to mind:

First of all, my harried, late arrival back on campus with the debate looming before me...then a frantic conference with Dow the afternoon before the occasion, the hasty, windy, effort to throw together an improvised case...the hectic dinner at the Union with Dr. Chapin with a few words of consolation bantered about (I had been sick during the afternoon, and could only handle tea and toast!)...the auditorium nearly filled with people, the Cal debaters with their card files and stacks of evidence, the chairman introducing the first speaker, the debate was on and I had nothing to say!

I mean that literally. Our few stock arguments I had given to Dow, and I was up against a purely impromptu address. I sat in a fog through the first half of the debate, but luckily inspiration struck just before I had to speak. The Cal men had pressed their case with relentless precision, not to speak of their appalling seriousness. They had spoken gravely in general terms, and it occurred to me that if we were to stand any chance at all, we must suddenly become light-hearted—humorous if possible—and specific. And so the address that sort of came to me while I talked (am I boring you, Darling?) proceeded along the following lines:

They had accused the unions of racial discrimination, and asked for legislation to prevent this practice. I remembered that racial discrimination is not limited to unions, but that, in fact, the unions are the most active of all our institutions in their attempt to correct it. I mentioned a Negro congress I had attended in San Francisco, and pointed out that there were no representatives of the Chamber of Commerce there, that management had not so much as sent an office boy, but that three very prominent labor union presidents were there, officiating on the platform. I reminded them of the vigorous efforts of the CIO and AFL to unionize the South now underway, and proceeding under the slogan (at this point I suddenly realized I didn't know the slogan and had to improvise quickly with a suitable one): Negro and White, Working Alike! I tried to show the futility of attempting to legislate against ignorance and prejudice by pointing to the 14th amendment, and to its manifest failure.

They had argued against the practice of closed memberships, and had urged legislation to prevent this. (By this time, I had warmed up to the talk, and many mental bulbs were flashing). I suggested, again, that the practice of closed membership was not confined to labor, but was in common usage by many of our most distinguished professions, Law and Medicine, that the practice arose out of the feeling of insecurity, the fear that a particular field would become overcrowded, that as long as labor was confronted with the specter of unemployment, they would continue to find means for limiting membership for their own protection, and if they were not allowed to achieve this end in the open market, then they would be forced to seek it in the black market. It is not enough, I argued, to blandly say, "We will legislate this abuse out of existence." We need to know how? Are we to provide in the law, I asked, that union membership will be open to all comers? Obviously this is impractical, since most of our unions are trade unions, and membership depends upon certain qualifications. If this were done, the gentlemen from California might well turn in their cars for repairs tomorrow, and get a plumber instead of a mechanic. This happened to a friend of mine, I smiled, and afterwards every time he stepped on the gas, hot, soapy water was flushed across the windshield. Are you then, I asked, to stipulate in the law a thousand different codes of qualifications for a thousand different trades? This would be insane, for techniques in trades rapidly change, and the provisions of such a law would be perpetually obsolete. And so the argument went. Dow immediately fell into the new spirit of our case. In fact, he was so completely caught up in the momentum of the thing that he---a sound Republican---referred to Herbert Hoover, the patron saint of the university, as "that man, living in another age." We won the debate. The California men gathered up their files, stuffed their books in their brief cases, and went home. And it was all over as quickly as it began.

Darling, I apologize for taking all this time, the better part of an afternoon, giving you a blow by blow description of the debate. But after I got started, I didn't know where to stop.

My schedule for the quarter is all straightened out now, and I'm about to make inquiry into the procedure to follow for making arrangements for the trip abroad. The G.I. Bill [$75 per month] I hear is good in England and elsewhere, so that may eliminate the first big obstacle in our path.

Remember, Darling, "Follow the fellow who follows a dream." I love you,

I do,

Frosty

"Women Are Urged to Save Democracy; Speakers at Patriotic Conference Stress National Problems Which Affect the Home."

N.Y. times 1/26/1947

Stanford
January 26, 1947

Darling,

Much to say and little time to say it—so once again I'll type a business letter in a very personal way. It is about time to start making definite arrangements concerning the wedding and the trip. I can begin now by giving you a little more concrete information than heretofore. The last day of final examinations at the end of Spring Quarter is Wednesday, June 11th. Commencement isn't until the following Sunday, the 15th, but I can easily arrange to have my degree forwarded by mail, and needn't remain for the ceremonies. My "availability" date will be the eleventh, I suppose.

Darling, I've been counting on you coming down sometime during the quarter. As a matter of fact, everybody seems to be counting on it. There is just one week when the trip would be—from the standpoint of serious involvement in studies down here—inadvisable, and that would be in the middle of next March during finals. Outside of that, I'll be waiting, if you give me forewarning, that is, expectantly with open arms. I'll show you the parts of San Francisco you haven't seen before.

Getting the silver sounds fine to me; it's just right in every detail. I think every-day silver should be as attractive in its way as guest silver, perhaps even more so since we'll have to live with it so intimately. No, darling, my house design does not begin with the kitchen; it begins with the bath.

You mentioned, but didn't enclose those two fortune slips from the cake you received down at Fong's [Tea Garden Restaurant in Boise] They may carry hidden omens, you know. Remember this business of three on a match, and the penny in the frying pan to make the hamburgers a success? I had quite a start the other night when I dreamed (this is open to devastating Freudian analysis) that I had married a stranger!

Yesterday Dave, Baker, Andrew, Fisher, and I took a trip south to Monterrey to visit Varda, a surrealist artist of prominence here on the West coast. It turned out to be a beautiful trip. We motored the distance in Dave's convertible with the top down, during a fresh and sunny afternoon. We idled for a time on the coast near Monterrey, climbing the sharp cliffs above the spewing surf, drinking in the raw and stolid beauty, until we were braced and drunk with the tonic of the sea. Then we went on to Varda's, and it was like walking through a looking-glass into a different world.

Varda, I found, is not a surrealist in the accepted sense, but rather a primitivist. He lives in a cavernous barn which has, he claims, a kind of "continuity with time." In the center of the main room there is a circular fireplace, the chairs about which are so built as to allow the sitter to lie back and observe the ceiling, the great mirrors on the wall, and the weird paintings jutting from the walls. The whole appearance of the place was so unreal in the failing light as to make me feel that I was the principal character of a strange and singular dream. Varda, his wife, the conversation, even the food (octopus), were all in character. It was quite a memorable trip.

Darling, please do all you can about arranging for, or finding out about the correct procedure for our trip. I'll get to work on it down here presently. The sooner we know definitely whether we'll be able to make it, the sooner I'll be able to set things straight concerning Harvard Law School. Perhaps, in both connections, Chase and/or D. Worth could be of help, but we'll need to know definitely about the trip before we can act definitely regarding law school. Tell me what you think about it.

I weathered through a minor crisis in the Speech and Drama Department down here last week. I had been invited to give the keynote talk at the Toastmaster's Club in Redwood City tomorrow evening, and had accepted on the understanding that I would deal freely, and without restriction, on the Chinese situation. When I learned later that the talk was to be a "travelogue," and that it was intended to be "neutral and non-controversial in nature," I withdrew my acceptance, and suggested they invited another in my place. This brought on a series of conferences which ended with the decision that I could speak on my own terms. I think this will hold for the rest of the year, and I'm glad to have the matter favorably and finally settled. One of the chief reasons, I think, that we will never avoid that final act of horror, an atomic war, is simply because whole societies are caught up and held fast in a spasm of timidity. Even our most liberal and advanced colleges quake at having the fragile myths attacked. They would rather see them laid open for dissection in the "hush-hush" chambers of the private conference room.

Well, darling, this has been a long letter. I do hope you will be coming down soon, and that you'll be writing often much sooner. Give my love to the folks, and I will save a big share for you.

Frosty

"McArthur Orders Election in Japan; Asks for Preparations 'as Soon as Possible' After Session of the Present Diet Ends."

New York Times 2/7/1947

Stanford
February 7, 1947

My Darling,

Our letters cross. You write me of your trip—the trip I've so looked forward to, and I write to come anytime but not the middle of March. Then circumstances intervene to make the date for you, and of course, it turns out to be the middle of March!

The big thing wrong with your date of arrival, Darling, wrong at least from point of view, and I hope yours as well, is that I won't even be in California, nor in the country for that matter: You see, I'll be in Hawaii.

You'll remember my telling you of my hopes of making the trip at Christmas. It is, with the traditional Joffre Debate, the big event of the forensic year. There was much fuss made over it early this quarter. The University wanted to make it a special "good will" tour, the Stanford alumnus in Hawaii has arranged for a series of banquets and side-trips to the outlying islands to coincide with the 40th anniversary celebration which will then be in progress, and the University of Hawaii has assumed a liberal portion of the expense of the trip. Well, the upshot of it all is that competitions were held and eliminations made, and Dow Carpenter and I were chosen for the trip. Now I learn that you will arrive on the coast while I am in mid-Pacific.

Bethy, I'll more than make up for my absence during your first week or so when I get back. Spring Quarter will be brand new with neither studies nor exams pressing, so we'll just make San Francisco our headquarters, and have a wonderful time. And, I'll escort you carefully about the campus, showing you all its flaws; we'll corner Spice for a good long visit and then compare notes on what's in prospect for Carl; and I'll drive you to some fantastic beauty spots above the Pacific. Who knows, in this season all of California is in a continuous park. If the winds are right and the spell is set, you might even agree to marry me. (In June of course. My fling, by agreement, is to run a full five months!)

Mother tells me you have a lovely new black suit, and that she is planning a birthday party for you on the 19th. She told me this in a casual way in the last letter, but her motive was to make sure I wouldn't forget it. Darling, will a valentine do?

Ask me to tell you about the D.A.R. in my next letter. There is a rare opportunity in the offing.

I love you,

Frosty

"China Reds Report 'Biggest Victory'; Seven Nationalist Divisions 'Annihilated' in Shantung."

N.Y. Times 2/27/1947

Stanford
February 27, 1947

My Darling,

A philosophy test is in the offing for tomorrow, and my notes and papers confront me with commanding impertinence. The end of mid-terms is just ahead, but finals loom in the next few weeks, all of which, by pre-arrangement, I must take early. There are book reports too, the inevitable book reports! Coupled with all this, are the different talks to be thrown in order for the Hawaii trip, together with the conferences, special arrangements, and passage papers to be arranged for. All of this is, as you might guess, plenty enough to keep me hopping.

On top of the pile, presently, lies the China talk. The well-fed matrons of San Jose, where nothing disturbing has occurred in the last decade, are pleasantly aroused by my teapot tempest on China, and they have taken whip in hand to prod their husbands into line. This has led to a splash of invitations recently which has turned me professional. Yesterday, the Rotarians paid me twenty-five dollars for a half-hour talk. Taking money from the Rotarians is practically as worthy a cause as damning the regime of Chiang Kai Shek. If I can manage to get things well enough organized, perhaps I'll be able to buy a dress suit for our wedding.

This is "Hell" week on the farm, the time when fraternity pledges get initiated. I may have told you of my displeasure with fraternities. Some of the practices that are now being flaunted are unbelievable. I've managed a working arrangement in the house that leaves me unmolested, but Carl has caused a great furor down at Kappa Sig that has been rather bitter at the edges. It seems that every time he misses a function, he gets fined, and he makes a point of missing all the functions. Since he has no money to pay the fines, consternation over the whole affair reigns at Kappa Sig.

Darling, every time I think about your coming down, I get more excited. There's so much we can do up and down the coast, and if you get here about the first of April, study will be no problem, and we can just play for a while.

They say the snow is going to melt soon at Yosemite. This weekend we're going up to take advantage of what's left. I can ski about as well as I can cook, but it ought to be lots of fun anyhow. I'll give you a fall-by-fall description next time I write.

The day I sent you my last letter (a note containing a letter to Worth) I received your latest from Salt Lake. Make this trip count, Darling. Be sure you get your money's worth. About the people who should receive invitations to the wedding, I will send a complete list as you suggested next week, including some indication of the likelihood of their attendance. Will that be soon enough?

Speaking of cooking, I saw a cook book on Chinese food at the college book shop today. If you run across one, why don't you pick one up. If you do, I'll get us a couple of pairs of ivory chop sticks.

That's all for now. Give my love to the folks, to Beulah and Jack, to the kids---this sounds like the end of a radio opera---

All my love, Darling, to you,

Frosty

"Gen. Chou En-lai, chief diplomatic figure of the Chinese Communists, bitterly charged today that the United States still was heavily supporting the Chiang Kai-shek Government and that American policy "has gone from bad to worse."

N.Y. Times 3/10/1947

March 10, 1947

Darling,

What a typist you're turning into! Do you manage it all without looking at the keys? Your letter---and this is really an exceptional quality for a typed letter---made me feel warm and cheerful, and made me hope that mine don't leave you frigid.

The trip to Yosemite was as spectacular as it was enjoyable. We were lucky enough to become the benefactors of four inches of new snow on Saturday, which made for wonderful skiing, as you can imagine on Sunday morning. I have enclosed a few pictures Spice took on the trip. The two people you won't recognize, Darling, are Brenchley, my roommate, and Spice.

I did make sense of that paragraph having to do with your trip down here. Bethy, if you get in before March 19th, by all means let me know. Dow and I leave on the clipper at 10:00, on the morning of the 19th, and if you're here I must see you before going. Phone me when you arrive, Palo Alto 8760. If you don't make it by the 19th, I'll be back on the Pan American plane, arriving at 6:00A.M. on the 1st of April, and will expect you at the airport. I will write you at the Lombard Hotel while I'm away.

Next quarter Carl and I will be rooming together over in Encino (that makes the cycle complete!) or in a private lodging house. But more of that later.

I'm awfully happy that you're coming down. It isn't only that we can have such fun, but also that we can make the arrangements for June and afterwards, which are still pending and stand badly in need of our attention.

The invitation list I have also—belatedly—enclosed, which brings me around to saying,

Darling, I love you,

Frosty

p.s. Chinese philosophy is almost as good as Chinese food.

"Democracy, Town Meeting Style; Those who have doubts about how democracy works should look to New England villages, where citizens keep their eyes on everything."

N.Y. Times 3/23/1947

March 23, 1947

Darling,

Just a note to let you know how things have gone. We had an unruffled flight out to the islands, arriving at about 7:30 in the evening at the Honolulu airport. There was a crowd of students at the airport from the University to welcome us with leis, kisses, and photographs. Certainly we were warmly received in the best Hawaiian traditions. Dow and I were then set up in an apartment just two blocks off Waikiki Beach---very convenient---which belongs to one of the students, Tom.... by name, who generously move in with a friend for the period of our stay.

Waikiki, I had been forewarned, would be a disappointment but it wasn't. On the contrary, it's a beautiful, and very fashionable beach where the water is so clear that the coral bed beneath is visible for a great distance, and the swimmers can wade out a quarter of a mile or more. The breakers roll in smoothly for great distance which makes the famous surf boarding possible. Dow and I were given guest cards at the Outrigger Club, next to the Royal Hawaiian Hotel, where the accommodations for bathing and playing on the beach are marvelous.

Our schedule has been very heavy, but before I give you a few of the high spots, let me tell you about the way Honolulu has turned into an "old home town."

The second night we were here, I ran into Dixon.... in his Ensign's uniform at the Queen's Surf, a very elegant night club on the beach. He had read about our arrival in the papers and had tried to contact me.

Then I received a telephone call---what a chatty call—from Mrs. Nourse, if you can imagine. We went all the way from Mary Anna to you back to Mary Anna again before I could get the receiver down, but she was very nice nonetheless. She and Dr. Nourse were present at the debate, and both seemed to enjoy it a great deal.

I still have my cousin to look up at Pearl Harbor and Helen .... friend at the McKinley High School.

Idaho was well represented at the debate Friday night. A Pam.... (?), who used to know me in high school, although as usual I didn't recognize her, was there to write an article for the

Statesman, while a couple of old friends from pre-war Stanford also showed up to make the reunion complete.

The debate itself was a much publicized affair out here. We seem to have turned up to face a tidal wave of Statism. They've asked for it 14 times in the past. This being the eve of their 15th attempt, feeling is running a little high. It's more of a crusade than a movement. The debate was attended by more than 1,000 in a hall so crowded that people were sitting in the aisles, and on the window sills, and many more were turned away for lack of space. The debate was broadcast, and the audience throughout was extremely enthusiastic.

I'll tell you privately, Darling, that we won the debate, but we lost the discussion. God himself couldn't have won the decision against Statehood. But it was a diplomatic triumph anyway. Everybody is so pleased now that Dow and I are feted about like distinguished ambassadors from a sovereign university. We surely haven't lacked attention.

We are going across the island today for a swim and a tour. Next week we go to Maui and then to Hawaii.

I wish you were here, Darling, even if that's the way it's supposed to be said on a post-card.

Love,

Frosty

Bethine Clark greeting Frank Church on his return from Honolulu.

> *"President Truman's stern emphasis on the need for "cooperation" by business, rather than regulation of it, was received today as additional evidence of the new approach being taken by the Administration toward private enterprise.*
>
> N.Y. Times 4/12/1947

April 12, 1947

Darling Bethy,

Here goes that veteran letter writer, swinging into another few pages of voluminous correspondence. How do you possibly find the time, Darling, to read the prodigious letters I send?

Has Anna called yet? If she hasn't, it's only because she hasn't gotten back yet. I do think, however, that it would be wise to look into this apartment prospect. The address Anna gave me is:

    Mrs. Barges D. Wayne (She is known only professionally as Dr. Margaret Addison)

       119 Hemingway, Apartment #15

       Boston, Mass.

Speaking of addresses, Mother was anxious to know my new one. Tell her that Encino Hall is sufficient, since I get my mail at General Delivery anyway.

Well, Darling, I've had a devil of a time trying to settle down since you left. From the looks of things, I'm going to be very busy for the rest of the quarter. That vacation we spoke of will certainly come as a welcome relief.

I'm glad you find it less satisfying without me, but it's a daring prophesy you make nonetheless. The chances are that your husband will become your biggest obstacle to untroubled living. But, then, I miss you too.

Give my best to the folks---and remember that

I love you, Darling

Frosty

"Prime Minister Stalin raised his vodka glass to propose the health of President Truman and Secretary of State Marshall toasted the future success of peacemakers tonight. This occurred as the Council of Foreign Ministers session ended in a gale of cordiality at a banquet in St. George's Hall of the Kremlin."

N.Y. Times 4/25/1947

April 25, 1947

Darling,

Last night I heard the foreboding story of the man without an apartment, footloose in San Francisco. Old Bluford was the man, the apartment took him on a week-long and wearisome guest. Fortunately, Dave had contacts (there are lots of Stanford men in San Francisco), and after enough pressure was brought to bear on the right realtors—the term now used to distinguish the profession---Bluford managed to get hold of the last flat in a newly-built set of five. It's unfurnished, and rents for $85.00 a month. He bought a $90.00 studio couch, the lone piece of furniture, and has moved in.

Stories like this bring me back with a start to the realization that you and I, Bethy, are going to be married in a scant two months, that we will be drifting across country, just as though everything was settled and waiting, and that we're going to finally find ourselves really up against it. I'm a little worried, Darling. Is there is any way we can get hold of a place by fortuitous pre-arrangement, we had better do so. What I'm saying, Bethy, is see what you can do. I haven't any way of doing much of anything from here.

Darling, have you noticed the convenient timeliness of this stationery? It's made to order for a person who wants to give the illusion that he is writing more than he actually is. Now that I've told you, I can't possibly fool you.

Last week I received a package from The Mode, Boise, filled with something I badly needed—as you know, my wardrobe is in pretty sad shape---best-quality handkerchiefs. There was no name or card, but I assume they came from you, or from your mother. In either case, I really appreciated them. They happened to arrive just as I dispatched my last handkerchief to the laundry. I was in a gay mood the rest of the day. Thanks a whole lot.

I've been listening to Richard Strauss tonight, and watching the crescent moon fade and clear as it passed behind the broken clouds. Isn't it commonplace to write about the moon—but somehow it was restful and comforting to watch it glide dreamily along tonight.

The days have been beautiful, in an almost unbroken procession, since you left Easter Sunday. It was unfair of the weather, wasn't it? Tomorrow, a few of us are going down to Carmel to spend the day on the beach. I'll miss the California sun in Boston [Frank and Bethine returned to Stanford after his freshman year at Harvard Law School] Darling, I'll have to rely entirely on your radiance. The brightness of the sun will be your smile, the warmth, your love.

Write to me soon,

Frosty

p.s. Somehow that name, "Frosty," doesn't accord well with the closing paragraph.

"Communist Influx Seen in All Fields; Hoover tells Congress Committee Percentage of Reds in U.S. is Higher than in Russia of '17."

N.Y. Times 5/6/1947

May 6, 1947

Darling,

Here I am—out of range of the rolling pin—and taking advantage by delaying a letter for more than a week.

The summer just has to roll around soon with you to soothe me back to health. This quarter is rapidly putting me under a bewildering mass of work. My chief hope is that, unlike Holmes' one-horse shay, I'll manage to hold together until I can turn myself over to your care come June. I'm going to require more attention than you, Darling. I'm going to be your patient.

There's a fat letter waiting, I suspect, at home for your return. This is written with the hope that it will reach you while you're still in the North, sometime before Mother's Day.

Haven't been able to locate a dark suit anywhere yet. California frowns on sober colors, but this must be a respectable wedding, and I'll find one somewhere.

As plans are shaping up, Spice won't be able to come to the wedding. She is very disappointed. She told me the other day---with evident delight—that she had received a letter from you.

But Carl, Bobby ...., Sammy ...., and I will probably leave on the night of the 12th, that is the early morning of the 13th, and drive straight through to Boise. Bobby has to be an usher at Marie.... wedding on the 14th, which will give him just enough time to get out of his car, change into his tux, and grope his way to the church.

So, as things look now, we will have a week or so together before the affair comes off, time for the ring and last minute arrangements.

How are things shaping up from your end, Darling?

Your last letter was sensational. I could picture Perry with Pat, and you with D. Worth, and Helen distracted by your late arrival —and even the sorrowful steak.

You had better keep me some distance away from Helen..... You know the weakness I show for Clarks. It's only exceeded by my notorious weakness for sophisticates.

My regards to the folks and my love to you, Darling.

Frosty

"Russia is Caustic on Policy in Japan; Says Occupation Has Led to 'Economic Blind Alley' as Council Feud is Renewed."

N.Y. Times 5/15/1947

Stanford University
May 15, 1947

Darling,

The way you flit about, I can't possibly keep track of you. Being a pretty bad correspondent at best, I must seem really terrible when my letters miss their mark and go astray. I have all the advantages, Darling. I stay relatively cemented in place, except for a few weekends and such, and your letters arrive securely to spread their cheer. This last letter, though, had the mark of the harried bride-to-be. Do you remember when I once wrote you and failed to sign? You said, "I don't mind the typing, but I'd like to know who the letter's from---for sure." Well, as I say, this last letter of yours carried the mark of the harried bride-to-be, for it lacked either a signature, or even a completed sentence. It ended this way:

Until I hear from you there are a million questions in my mind about things I should do, but this is more-or-less to tell you that things happened in such a hurry, and that......????

Now I've been thinking about all the possible endings to that sentence. Some are reassuring, some are foreboding, and some are positively terrifying---and I mean that with two s's. So, Darling, you must write and explain, just to give me rest.

The car sounds very handsome, and I'm awfully happy you're so pleased with it. Mother also wrote about it in glowing terms. She ended her letter with a suggestion that perhaps the two of you could drive down to the graduation, giving the car its maiden voyage, and then we could all drive back together. This would be wonderful, but there is a time factor that enters in to complicate things a bit. I don't think I had planned on staying for the formal graduation exercises, since commencement isn't until the 15th, and we probably wouldn't arrive home until the 17th. That would rush things a bit, don't you think? The present plan is to leave for home on the 13th, but if you could come down just for the ride early, it would certainly be swell. Well, anyway, arrange things anyway you can, because you're going to be the busy one, and I'll act accordingly.

Darling, I'm sure your letter to Ann.... was more than adequate.

This last week has been a scorcher. Somehow, all my midterms together with the preliminary and final competitions for the annual Joffre Debate, all came at the same time. I managed to pass the exams---however not with flying colors by any means---and to be chosen as one of three members of the Stanford team for the debate. The debate will be held on the 26th of this month here at Stanford.

Just five more weeks to go, Darling. It's like saying "thirty five days until Christmas!"

All my love,

Frosty

"At the rate at which German denazification courts are proceeding, Gen. Lucius D. Clay said today, they will require several years to dispose of the vast number of cases still pending before them in the United States occupation."

N.Y. Times May 17, 1947

Stanford University
May 17(?) 1947

Darling,

Here comes the typewritten letter.

I have the same trouble you've often complained of, Bethy. I can think of a myriad of things to tell you, but when it comes to putting them down in writing, my mind goes suddenly blank. The best answer, I think is just to chat at random for a while.

Perhaps I've mentioned that Bay and Bluf were disappointed not to have the chance to see you. Brench wanted to get to know you better, and loudly protested the briefness of his chance meeting the night of your hectic arrival. Bluf blew in from Chicago in a frenzy of bluff exuberance. He seems to have run the gauntlet of political inclinations, having now completed the cycle of placing himself back within the grip of the North Shore. His newest hobby is wire recording. He has a recorder promised as a wedding present, and one of his projects is that of recording my addresses "for posterity." This is a flattering sentiment, but naturally, we won't ever quite get around to doing it. I'm sure "posterity" won't object.

Bay's new convertible---he did manage to get it in a last-minute concession from this mother—will probably be the death of him. He's managed two accidents in two weeks, something of a record, and the car, as a consequence, has been in the garage so consistently that I haven't seen it yet. Paris is in the offing, however, so he's happily looking forward to next year with rosy anticipation. I can't blame him; it should prove an exciting and memorable year.

Carl has had rough sliding in two different connections since you left. First of all, although he had been one of ten finalists competing for a University trip abroad this summer, he failed the final selection of two men. He had rough competition—the two men who were chosen were both graduate students---and did well to go so far, but it was a disappointment nonetheless. Actually I think it will turn out for the best, because it will give Carl an opportunity to work this summer and to save a little money.

The second episode is equally to his credit, but again ends as a disappointment. Carl was persuaded to make the run for student body president. [Carl Burke was the chairman of Frank Church's Senate and Presidential campaigns]. His chances looked respectable, and I gave him moderate encouragement, at any rate, to run. I suppose, Darling, that any advice that leads to embroilment in campus politics is ill-advised. Still, the presidency is the one office that can be of real benefit to its occupant in terms of the experience and the contacts. Well, to shorten an otherwise long story, the primaries were held yesterday in which eleven candidates competed for the nominations. Four were nominated for the finals next week, while Carl narrowly missed out by placing a close fifth.

[end of letter missing]

"Russia Stands Pat. Mr. Gromyko has stated once more Russia's thesis on atomic weapons and general disarmament. The net result is a reiteration of his Government's demand that the United States disarm first by abandoning atomic bombs..."

N.Y. Times 5/21/1947

May 21, 1947

My Darling,

I don't know whether to be more impressed by your amazing efficiency, Bethy, or by your very understandable consternation. But I think, if I weren't going to marry you, I would quite probably employ you as my private secretary. You have done beautifully with arrangements that will prove, I feel, important later on. Darling, you're doing yourself proud.

Let me see, now, all I have to do is make the decisions. This is the flattering duty that every male since Adam covets and sometimes has only the illusion of performing. In this case, however, the details are so clear, and the facts bearing on the various matters so evident, that the decisions are more pleasant than burdensome. I'll hazard a few.

First of all, don't feel badly about the mistaken spelling on the invitation. I have always secretly felt that Forrester ought to be spelled with only one "r" anyway. Insisting upon two "r's" is very much like spelling Smith with a "y." As for being at home on Idaho Street, I think I'll feel very much at home there, although we probably won't quite make it by the tenth.

The letter from Mrs. Wayne is certainly encouraging, and I think we should let her know we are interested in getting one of the apartments in Cambridge. I doubt if we could do better on our own. We should put in a claim for one as soon as possible on the understanding that we will arrive in Boston the first week in September.

It seems that all you have to do, Bethy, is drop a hint and people go to work for you. This room that Camille.... recommends in Mexico City sounds ideal. Mexico City ought to be headquarters. If there is room enough for the both of us (I would resent a separation), and if the food is good, I see no reason for not taking advantage of the quarters. It occurred to me that we might stop off in New Orleans on the way down and then perhaps come back by way of California. This schedule would put us in Mexico City no earlier than ten days following the wedding. I think you'd be safe in writing to that effect.

I'll check on the typhoid shots. Thanks for the reminder. And incidentally, Darling, salmon sounds fine. But, to my knowledge, no passport is needed to get into Mexico. The arrangement is like that pertaining to American travel in Canada.

Spice told me today that she was writing to tell you that she will be able to attend the wedding. She's delighted, and of course, so is Carl.

Yesterday evening, Bay, Carl, and I managed to get seats at the San Francisco Opera House for the great rally in honor of Henry Wallace. The hall was crowded with over 4,000 people, while a cheering throng of equal size milled about outside the building. Wallace received a standing ovation from the audience. I liked him. I liked his fighting spirit, his frankness, and his great sincerity. It was an exciting affair.

This seems to cover the business of the moment. I note by the date that his is sort of an anniversary in reverse---there is just one month left to the day.

I love you,

Frosty

[Frank Church was awarded the Joffre Medal for debate at Stanford University]

WESTERN UNION

PALO ALTO CALIF

MISS JEANNE BETHINE CLARK

109 IDAHO STREET

BOISE IDA

UNDESERVING BUT LUCK GOOD. WON JOFFRE MEDAL. FRENCH CONSUL GENERAL INFORMS THAT NEWS CARRIED PARIS PAPERS WEDNESDAY. VIVE LA FRANCE. LOVE, FROSTY

"Chiang Lays War to Chinese Reds; Bars Government Overtures—Other Developments Appear to Block Parleys Now."

New York Times 5/30/1947

Stanford
May 30, 1947

Darling,

Another one of those crisp business notes, and again overdue. I appreciated your telegram, Darling. It was very thoughtful of you not to leave me unattended last Monday. As it was, I had fallen heir to a bad chest cold that kept me in bed over the weekend and most of Monday. It was really quite a funny situation, if it hadn't been for the fact that I was anxious to win the debate, since I could hardly navigate, and was on the point of losing my voice at any moment. But the Fates were good, and I managed to avoid both the spasms of uncontrollable coughing I had anticipated, and loss of voice until after the debate ended.

I sent the folks the newspaper accounts of the affair which give the details I needn't repeat here. The medal itself is quite a prize. In pre-war years, each was struck off in the government mint in France, but with the difficulty and confusion of recent years it has been designed and cast each year in San Francisco. It is a large and heavy silver medallion, engraved with a striking representation of Marshall Joffre, and inscribed on one side with the words: "J. Joffre, Marechal de France," and on the other: "Ministere des Affaires Etrangeres."

When I collected my mail yesterday, there was among the envelopes on carrying the return-address, "Aloha Crafts," and looking suspiciously as if it might be from Anna. Of course it was. Anna had sent the menus from the Matsonia she had promised! Every time I look at them I can see her ordering for

Robert—right down to the last toothpick. Anna said the wedding invitations are "quite the talk of the town," and that "she and Robert would certainly be there with bells on. Ah yes, dear Anna!

But that brings me around to invitations. I don't think Dow has received his, although I think he ought to get one. There is also a problem with relation to Don…, my third roommate. I included his name on one of the lists I sent you. He feels very much left out. In fact, despite the distances, he might even come. This would make for complications---housing and the like in Boise--- but I suppose it isn't very gracious to live with him for three months and not extend him an invitation. There are a couple of additions I should make to the announcement list too, without the "at home" cards. ...

Sammy Dunford—He'll get home about the time I do, I think. If the announcements go out earlier, his Stanford address is [provided].

Darling, I promise to sound less business-like when I get home. If there are things I should take care of down here, or if I can help out in any way, let me know and I'll do my best. Finals begin a week from today, and as I've warned you, I'm just the hollow frame of my former self. That's pretty bad when you consider how little there was to start with! You could find better specimens without any trouble at all, Bethy, but for my sake don't look around for any.

My love to your mother, and tell Chase I appreciate his inquiries regarding the license and the other details which, had I been left to find out about after I got home, would probably have turned our June wedding into a July apology.

Every time I read over one of these letters I'm appalled by the fact that it isn't until the very end that I get around to saying,

I love you,

Frosty

"Senate to Receive Borah Statue."

N.Y. Times 6/6/1947

June 6, 1947

Darling,

Your last letter was certainly wonderful. I think you know me pretty well, for you certainly know just what to say to cheer me up. As for the fairy tale, Bethy, my only real concern is that I'm likely to be more of a Prince Alarming than a Prince Charming when I get home.

I think Phyllis…. should be invited by all means, and probably Bobby….as well. Yes, it's true Darling that every time I write there's a change in plan, but of those we've asked down here, Don, Brench, Baker, Bluford, and Dow, only Carl and Spice will be able to make it. Bluf still talks about it, but a job with the airlines is going to tie him down. So, Bethy, there should be space.

You had better address the invites to the Boise address of both Phyllis and Bob.

Lots of love,

Frosty

On June 21, 1947, Frank and Bethine Church were married at the Clark family's Robinson Bar Ranch on the Salmon River in Idaho.

After their marriage, the Churches returned to Boise where Frank Church practiced law and began planning his campaign for the U.S. Senate in 1956.

Church narrowly defeated former Senator Glen Taylor in the Democratic primary and then defeated the Republican incumbent Senator Herman Welker. At age 32, he became one of the youngest Senators elected to office.

During his first term. he was appointed to serve on the Senate Foreign Relations Committee that Senator William Borah of Idaho chaired during the early 20th century. After serving some 20 years on the Committee, Church finally became Chairman in 1979.

Frank Church with Deng Xiaoping, Vice Chairman, Chinese Communist Party during his visit to Washington, D.C. in January, 1979.

March 15, 1979 – Senator Frank Church announced today that he will lead a delegation of several members of the Senate Foreign Relations Committee to China in April. Church is chairman of the committee. Scheduled to accompany Church on the trip are Senator Jacob Javits of New York, the ranking Republican on the committee, and Senators Joseph Biden of Delaware, Paul Sarbanes of Maryland, and Edward Zorinsky of Nebraska.

At the same time a separate delegation of...business leaders is expected to visit the mainland for talks with trade officials...the two groups will coordinate their itinerary in Peking. Both delegations will be visiting China at the official invitation of the Chinese government."

Senators Frank Church and Joe Biden with Robert Pedersen, President of Ore-Ida Foods, then based in Idaho, who chaired the trade mission that accompanied the Senate delegation to China in 1979.

January 23, 1980 – Senator Frank Church, the chairman of the Senate Foreign Relations Committee, said today conferring "most favored nation" status on China would open the doors to further trade markets for the United States."

Excerpts from Frank Church Speech "The Quest for Peace Must Continue" at the Fund for Peace in N.Y. City 11/17/1979:

"Nearly 40 years ago, I thought the world had learned a lesson. I was then a Lieutenant in the U.S. Army, stationed in Kunming, deep in the remote interior of China. It was there during the final phase of World War II, I first heard the startling news that the United States had detonated an atomic bomb. There at the foot of the Himalayas, we gathered in our barracks to hear broadcasts from afar about mushroom clouds of searing heat, deadly radiation, and the dust of disintegrating cities filling the skies above Japan.

"To be sure, the obliteration of Hiroshima and Nagasaki signified an early end to the war. For this, we were thankful. But nearly everyone in uniform I knew in Kunming believed that we had entered a new age, where war itself would wither away. Logically, since war represented an organized assertion of force to achieve obtainable national objectives, atomic war seemed unthinkable. What rational purpose could be served by the total destruction of all combatants? Obviously, nations just emerging from the dreadful bloodbath of the Second World War would have to find a way to settle their disputes peacefully in the future. The atom bomb, so it seemed, had made war obsolete...

"Every citizen who loves this country, its freedom and good life; every parent whose children yearn for their day in the sun; every American who believes our national heritage still *represents 'the last, best hope on earth,' must become earnestly engaged in the active quest for peace."*

This last paragraph is engraved on the grave marker of Frank Church in Boise's Morris Hill cemetery

In 1980, Senator Church was defeated for-re-election to a fifth term. He then joined the Washington, D.C. office of the law firm, Whitman and Ransom until his death in 1984.

Excerpts from Frank Church speech "The United States and China: A New Relationship to be Kept in Perspective," Sears Lecture Series, Purdue University, 2/22/1982:

"I, myself, while liking the Chinese people and admiring their ancient culture, am an adherent to Western values. I believe in individual liberty, democratic government, and the free market. I'm satisfied with the free enterprise system and content to leave to the Chinese the evolution of their particular brand of communism.

'The last time I was in China, I witnessed the many splendors of the Forbidden City; the awesome ruins of the Great Wall; and the amazing engineering feat of the Grand Canal. These are spectacular antiquities, to be sure, but antiquities all the same.

"Crossing over from China to Japan was like leaping out of the past into the future. Upon arriving at the Okura Hotel in Tokyo, my wife, Bethine, and I experienced a kind of culture shock. Our room was cast in soft lamp light, the curtains drawn behind a bouquet of beautiful flowers. On the table, a bottle of wine, with two gleaming glasses and a serving of excellent cheese, had been placed, while freshly washed bathrobes and slippers were carefully laid out upon the beds. Bethine went at once to shower, filling the bathroom with luscious steam. When she finished, she returned, propped herself up against two fluffy pillows, reached for her wine glass, cut herself a slice of cheese, and began to enjoy the delightful music which filled the room.

"Then she smiled, looked at me and said, 'Thank God for capitalism!'"

Frank and Bethine Church in Beijing's Forbidden City in 1979.

Senator Frank Church was Chairman, Senate Foreign Relations Committee (1979-1981) and Senate Select Committee on Intelligence (1975-1976).

Made in the USA
Middletown, DE
27 June 2024